INDEX

INTRODUCTION 4

DEDICATION 7

Running from Perpetual Loneliness 9

Into the Darkness 26

The Inverted World 37

To be Sealed 50

Being Raised by God 62

The Valley of Decisions 77

40 Days in the Wilderness 96

Delivered 109

Sealed 117

The Assignment 128

ACKNOWLEDGEMENTS 135

ABOUT THE AUTHOR... 136

INTRODUCTION

As I wake up every morning, the first words out of my mouth are always, 'good morning Heavenly Father'. I feel His presence covering me and the warmth of His love all around me. He always makes sure I sleep soundly. As I get up, I look into the mirror and I say, 'there you are' with the biggest smile on my face – for it was once, in a prayer to my Heavenly Father, that I saw myself the way He sees me. From then on, I saw my childlike spirit, my eagerness to serve and the glow that always appeared on my cheeks as I smiled. I always make my coffee just the way I like it with the creamiest raw milk I can buy in the village, a touch of cinnamon and a sprinkle of black salt – a little delicacy that a dear sister in Christ, the Duchess, once taught me.

Every morning is luxurious with my Heavenly Father, so I always pour my coffee into my delicate, English Rose Royal Albert tea cup with its matching saucer and golden spoon. I drink it slowly with Him, for every moment with Him is precious. I move slowly as I read through His choice of Bible chapters that day and fully indulge in the softness, the safety and the love of my Heavenly Father. I shower and dress myself, making sure I choose the garments that best represent His generosity and His glory.

Signed • Sealed
DELIVERED

A woman's ascension from the bottomless pitt to the Heavenly Kingdom

By
Laura Ansell

MAPLE
PUBLISHERS

Signed Sealed Delivered : A woman's ascension from the bottomless pitt to the Heavenly Kingdom (room for change)

Author: Laura Ansell

Copyright © Laura Ansell (2025)

The right of Laura Ansell to be identified as author of this work has been asserted by the author in accordance with section 77 and 78 of the Copyright, Designs and Patents Act 1988.

First Published in 2025

ISBN 978-1-83538-721-4 (Paperback)
      978-1-83538-722-1 (Hardback)
      978-1-83538-723-8 (E-Book)

Cover designed by katieamanda.com

Book layout by:
   White Magic Studios
   www.whitemagicstudios.co.uk

Published by:
   Maple Publishers
   Fairbourne Drive, Atterbury,
   Milton Keynes,
   MK10 9RG, UK
   www.maplepublishers.com

A CIP catalogue record for this title is available from the British Library.

All rights reserved. No part of this book may be reproduced or translated by any form or by any means, electronic or mechanical, including photocopying, recording or by any information storage and retrieval system without written permission from the author.

The views expressed in this work are solely those of the author and do not reflect the opinions of Publishers, and the Publisher hereby disclaims any responsibility for them. This book should not be used as a substitute for the advice of a competent authority, admitted or authorized to advise on the subjects covered.

There's always something particularly special about the way I choose to do my hair. As I move my brush through it, it seems to have a particular feeling of comfort, so I do this with tenderness. As I choose the right bow for the back of my hair, I am reminded that I am still a child in His eyes. Just like our parents see us as children even as we move well into adulthood, so does He. I will always be a child in His eyes and, as I place the bow in its rightful place, I smile and He smiles back, warming up the whole room. He has taught me that His children are gifts in this world and gifts are always wrapped in a bow.

One morning recently, as I was getting myself ready for Him, the idea of this book moved into my heart. I had spent the night before in prayer, which consisted of me sobbing over a vintage handkerchief because of how magnificent He is but so many won't listen. I want everyone to know Him and move under His covering so that they no longer have to think that a life of anxiety, depression, medication, poverty and tiredness is normal. The love I felt for Him that night was so huge in my heart that I had to proclaim it and He heard it all. The very next morning, as I slowly prepared for His day, I heard Him say, 'write me letters.' My face beamed at the idea. What a wonderful way to express my love for Him. I started writing Him letters right away.

However, I must bring to the forefront that it was not me who wrote the pages of this book, for I can assure you that I'm not able to write with such romance. It's the Holy Spirit that dwells deep within me that writes with such elegance, therefore I take credit only for sitting down and obeying as to when and where to write. The stories that you will read about are indeed mine, but you'll see the Holy Spirit weaving Himself throughout the steps I took as a young girl to a young woman and now, an adult, humbled by the Lord as His servant.

I wish not to be served for I am not here for worldly gifts, only Heavenly gifts. The Lord has taught me better than to work hard for possessions or to be placed on a pedestal for others to gaze. I seek none of that. I receive only my blessings from heaven for I know that what I receive from heaven is mine forever. I seek not to grab attention or to chase that which I could have only for a fleeting moment, for I wish not to take even a shoestring unless presented to me by the Lord.

I therefore pass this book to you in the hope that, with the Holy Spirit, you shall indulge in it, knowing full well that those who are yet to receive the heart of Christ will read this, scoff and return to seeking more of Satan's flattery. I can only pray that one day, their eyes will be opened to the truth of our Lord and Saviour, Jesus Christ.

Thank the Lord that He has called me into writing this book. I hold so much love for Him that if I keep it contained any longer I may burst.

DEDICATION

This book is an utter devotion to God (my Heavenly Father – Papa). It is my love letter to Jesus, my Lord and saviour, and to the Holy Spirit, my dearest companion.

Laura Ansell

This is the testimony of a woman who can see beyond the real world. From a young age, Laura could see things that others couldn't and this book is written from the perspective of her eyes.

In the bible this was known as a seer.

Running from Perpetual Loneliness

WITH EYES TO SEE

No one will ever know how much I love the Holy Spirit. If it wasn't for Him taking ownership of my life, I'd still be the empty, lonely young lady who I once was. The way I describe that loneliness is by comparing it to the feeling of floating up in space with no way to come back to Earth and no way to die. This feeling of living in such an untethered abyss was a daily occurrence for me. It haunted me and made me want to run as far away from it as I could.

As I got older, I started to become bold with the ways that I could run away from it. I'd travelled a lot and lived in more than thirty houses. I'd experienced failed relationship after failed relationship, rarely feeling claimed but instead, used. I'd practiced meditation, breath work, yoga, inner healing, regression, reiki, mirror work and anything else one may think of to heal. I'd done it all but nothing could shift the perpetual loneliness the way my Heavenly Father did that one day.

The loneliness I was experiencing was the gap in my life where He should have been, though for so long I could not find Him. I did not know Him and the night time was the loneliest. If I could sleep with music on, I would, just so that I didn't have to feel the emptiness and hear the demons in the dark.

As a young child, there were lots of things I used to see. My grandmother said I had eyes like saucers. She was right, I do have big eyes. All the better to see you with. I also have big ears so I can hear what others can't. It was probably these abilities that made me love all things creative because I could see beauty where others couldn't. I didn't understand maths, I didn't care about science but I did love to draw, paint and create any chance I could. My mother always allowed me to dress myself as soon as I was able to do it. I'd spend time matching the bow in my hair to the frill on my sock and I enjoyed each morning where I could indulge in my outfit of the day. My nails were often painted, as were the nails of whoever entered the house, thanks to me. Creativity made me feel alive and God created my features to show the world the abilities that I had – I had eyes to see and ears to hear. I had the ability to bring heaven to earth.

He also gifted me with obedience. I would follow my mother quietly wherever she went. According to her, women would comment on how well I behaved and she was deeply saddened when it was time for me to start school. She missed my presence, as I missed hers, but my ability to obey would one day serve my Heavenly Father.

Finally, He gifted me with stubbornness. I moved to the beat of my own drum, and if you could ask my mother, she'd tell you that I never listened to her advice and instead always discerned my own path. He made me want to move in a direction that was against this world, and although this would serve Him in the future, it was certainly very difficult in my youth.

My large saucepan eyes saw lots of things, especially at night. As I would tuck myself into bed after having a bedtime story, and start to feel the presence of things coming into the room. They'd walk around the bed and move the floorboards. They'd sit at the end of the bed or on the wicker chair that I had in the corner of my room. I'd hear the wicker move and concave with their presence. The bedsheets would get tugged at and my face would get poked. One night, when I was particularly tired, I got angry at something pulling on my bed sheets. I bolted upright and shouted for them to stop, only to be met with the sound of my CD rack crashing to the floor.

I will never forget the worst night, for it kept me awake until the sun came up. I was woken up in the night by the sight of a young girl sitting on my floor and propped up against the wall. She had long blonde hair, which was braided into pigtails that hung over her shoulders and down her front, covering a grey dress. She wore white tights and black buckled shoes, and the positioning of her body was terrifying to me. Her head rested to one side and her toes fell inwards. To me, she looked dead. Terrified, I pulled the covers over my head and stayed there until the birds sang their morning lullabies. From that moment on I was afraid of the dark.

It was common knowledge in my family that the house we were living in was haunted. We thought it was ghosts, but now I know that we were being harassed by demons. A psychic once told my mother that it was just children playing, but this was my first experience of demons posing as something innocent so that my mother's compassion kept the door open to them.

When I was a teenager, I was allowed to have a small TV in my room, which I played all night so I could have some light in the room and drown out the noise. But by this time, I was already suffering mentally and physically. I had no clue who I was or why I was here, and this left me with a constant feeling of searching. I was to become a wandering soul.

SEEKING CONTROL

I had my first panic attack when I was fifteen years old, driving home from a shopping mall with my mother. Suddenly my lungs closed, my chest tightened, and I couldn't get air into my body. She panicked, I panicked and we called for an ambulance. They told me that I was having a panic attack. I didn't know much about panic attacks but it set me up for three months of hibernation. I was so afraid that I'd have another panic attack outside the house that I just didn't want to leave. I started to get into a habit of seeking comfort, which led to a form of slothfulness. I wasn't becoming a good steward of my life by taking ownership but instead, became the victim.

> **Each of you should use whatever gift you have received to serve others, as faithful stewards of God's grace in its various forms.**
> *1 Peter 4:10*

Of course I was wrong to develop a victim mindset, but it was all I could focus on at the time. God has given me the beautiful ability to be able to focus on whatever I love – if I love it, I can focus on it. If I loved you, I could focus on you. He made me this way for a reason. And until I found that reason, my focus went on to all the wrong things. At that time, I was fixated on safety and comfort. I needed to have some sort of control over my life as I felt so lost and, one day, I finally found the enemy's replica of control in a fashion magazine on the kitchen table.

When I opened it, there was an article all about eating disorders and how being size 0 was becoming a trend amongst teenagers. This magazine posted about websites in which young girls were encouraging each other to starve themselves. And so, of course, at sixteen years old, I was curious.

From the moment I went on the internet and typed in the website name, I was sent into eighteen months of starvation. I was focused and it felt so good to have something to focus on. It was all I knew – to deceive, to lie and to hide, just like Satan. He was, after all, the one who I was following without knowing it. Until, one day, I couldn't take it anymore and I sought out my father for help, as I so often did. He sent me to a therapist who let me unravel the things that were weighing heavy in my heart, which was mainly the loneliness and longing to fit in somewhere.

I'd had some friends here and there, but I struggled to really connect with people. Although the problem showed itself on the surface, the problem was supernatural. The eyes that God gave me to see, saw all sorts of things, and the one thing I really didn't understand was the golden light. Everyone has one and it would move right in front of them. When people followed it, I would feel relief from them; but when they didn't, I'd see stress and struggle. I couldn't understand why they didn't just follow that light. But then again, it appeared that I was the only one who could see it.

This made it difficult for me to be able to be totally genuine with people and, looking back, it may have made me socially awkward. But that is how demons scheme.

For our struggle is not against flesh and blood, but against the rulers, against the authorities, against the powers of this dark world and against the spiritual forces of evil in the heavenly realms.

Ephesians 6:12

Not only was I getting attacked in my sleep, but now they attacked me in the day also, and they used women. These women would chase me around at school and try to intimidate me. It worked. I'd make loops around the school, pretending I had somewhere to go for an hour, just so no one knew that I was friendless. I'd hide myself in the ladies room cubicles along with any lunch or snacks I had, just so that no one knew I had no one to eat with.

You can imagine that, by the time I was sixteen, after going through all this, I was more lost than ever. Satan had lined me up to take his bait and I did. I became interested in watching TV shows and movies that starred a witch. I was so drawn to their ability to own a room. They were confident because of the power they had and I wanted that power for myself. I sought out spell books, cauldrons, pentagram wall hangings, and anything that made me connect to the confidence that they had.

I had taken a turn of rebellion and, to look at me, you'd say I was a pretty troubled child. But in reality, I had a safe and loving home. My hair was black. My clothes were black. My nails were black. My make up was black. I had taken a turn of rebellion and Satan had used my God-given gift to move against the crowd, and against me. I was a gothic, skinny, hermit, who was about to graduate from school and be thrown into the world.

THE OLDEST LIE IN THE BOOK

As I was always the art kid, going to college meant that I could explore photography, art and design, so my few years in college helped me to come out of a dark place because I was able to channel my creativity into art. I photographed everything and everyone. I drew when I could. I painted when I could. I spent all my time in the art room, including my lunch breaks. I'd get in early and I'd leave late again. My ability to focus served me throughout college and it served me throughout university where I was able to get a degree in fashion and textiles.

My three years in university were difficult. Getting a degree is difficult in general, but to be making garments for fashion weeks that I rarely got to showcase felt extremely disheartening. I found myself once again in the classroom surrounded by people who I never felt liked me, though I could not put my finger on why. I often kept to myself. I was polite and had good mannerisms as my parents had raised me to have, yet something in me seemed to irritate others greatly.

Not understanding this, I took it personally and created so many identities to bend myself into what I thought they wanted me to be. But nothing worked. It just sent me into a darker hole. This seemed to be a problem that I would encounter many times in my life, and a problem that would only go away when I finally closed the door for the enemy. But here I was a twenty-five-year-old student finishing up her degree, feeling emptier than ever. I had lots of beautiful things in my life. The main thing being a relationship with a man who was my best friend. His name was Henry. He was a 6"6, motorbike instructor from the country and I loved him with all I had. We lived in a little house on his mother's property. It used to be a chicken shed, but they had converted it into a home. It was small and humble with one kitchen, one living room, one bedroom, and one bathroom.

As a woman, I did my best to turn it from a house into a home. Henry sometimes worked late shifts and I'd find myself cooking for him at 10pm many evenings in the summer. Every night without fail, I'd be so excited to hear his motorbike pull up in the driveway. There wasn't a day that went by where I didn't find myself immediately getting up and waiting by the front door to open it and greet him with a massive hug. I couldn't help myself. Life lit up when he was near and it only felt like a home when he was in it.

But after four years in that relationship something started to nag at me. The emptiness was still there and, although I felt it less in his presence, it was getting heavier and heavier.

I thought it was because I needed to be successful. I needed to make something of myself. I needed to be more. My father's ambition ran through my veins on a daily basis. I had such fire and hunger for life and I didn't know what to do with it.

Henry was different to me. He was humble. He was a simple man. He loved his family. He loved the country he lived in and had no intention of going anywhere. He had a peace that I just didn't. Over the four years of our relationship, it began to act as a divide. My constant longing for answers turned into more ambition. With this desire to go and see the world, and him with the desire to walk to our local pub, hand in hand, have a pint for himself and a glass of wine for me, a few chips and stroll back home, we seemed to be on different pages sometimes. But some of my favourite memories of him are sitting in the pub garden just talking the night away. Of course that was because of my emptiness, being so painful I had to find something to fill it.

One evening, we found ourselves at a dinner party for a friend's birthday. A woman with long brown hair and beautifully manicured nails leaned over to me and told me that a friend had told her that I was unhappy. I explained to her that there was just something in me that was longing for something that I didn't even understand.

Her response was, "Have you not read the secret?"

I shook my head.

In pure, snake-like fashion, she lured me into a mystical world of greener pastures if only I read this book.

I bought it and read it the next day. I bought the movie and watched that too. I asked my boyfriend if he'd watch it with me, but he didn't want to. I asked if he would read it. He didn't want to. I asked if I could read it to him. He didn't want to hear it.

But from the moment I read that book, he would say that was the day he lost me. According to him, I changed. Satan had taken my God-given gifts and used them against me. I became focused on the lie of manifestation and the law of attraction. I was on fire for it. I was the creator of my own reality. I was essentially, God. I could have what I wanted and be what I wanted if only I could just visualise and focus on what it was that I wanted. And so a new world began.

About six months later, I found myself separating from Henry. It was such a sad day. We had finally moved into a new house where we felt like we were slowly starting to make our way in the world. I'd finished university and was about to start a job in the fashion industry, but I found myself back at my mum's house crying over a broken heart for months and months. I longed for Henry and I waited for him. Not only did I miss him as my partner, but I missed him as my best friend. There was a divide between us that I couldn't put my finger on, but I knew it was there, and it was painful to see it.

Eventually, I moved on with my life, and decided that if I was single and didn't have responsibilities the way I used to, I could be free. I figured I could finally go to New York and could finally take the clothing pieces that I'd so carefully created and display them in the shops. I had a dream that I wanted my clothing line to be seen. I had graduated and created a twenty-five-piece collection. I was so awfully proud of it. It was a lot of work, but it was beautiful and I wanted the world to see it. So I quit my job, jumped on a plane and took it over to the Big Apple.

There, I was met with the coldness of New York streets. I set up meetings with merchandisers and fashion gurus, but no one seemed interested in my measly little twenty-five-piece collection. I stayed there for three months and, in that time, I found myself meeting a distinguished gentleman. He seemed wise and knowledgeable. He seemed self-assured. He was ambitious too. He seemed to be everything I needed.

However, when we started a relationship, and as I began to know him, and as he flew me back and forth to see him in America, it didn't take long for me to realise that we were not compatible. Of course I didn't want to get a broken heart again. I also knew that I had this 'secret' ability to focus, so surely, if I could create my own reality, I could create a beautiful and harmonious relationship with this man.

My family and friends soon lost me to a world of delusion.

TO SEE BEYOND

My God-given hyper-focused ability went towards making this man become what I needed him to be and making myself what he needed. I was good at adapting myself to fit in. I had actually become quite good at it.

One day, I found myself watching a tarot card reading on YouTube. I was amazed. Everything she said about a relationship applied to me. I was hooked. I had found Satan's peace – a short and temporary feeling of hope.

I wanted the power that she had because it reminded me of the power I sought after as a teenager amongst all the cauldrons and spell books. So I wandered into a local store and bought my very own deck of tarot cards. It was surprisingly easy to find such a tool. I took it home. I opened the cards and thumbed all the way through them. I could taste control. I loved the smell of the cards. Something felt powerful. I laid them out and took a few glances at them. Before I knew it, something in me just knew how to read them. My life took off in a whole new direction as people would come to me for readings on a regular basis. Before I knew it, I decided to create my very own YouTube channel where I could read tarot for anyone.

A year later I was completely dishevelled. I was working with five clients a day, six days a week, and I had an eight-month waiting list. But pride was the next sin that I began exploring. My ego got bigger as I had created a world where I finally felt needed. But there was a big price to pay: I was exhausted and empty, and the emptiness only felt bigger as I was now in a position to have the worldly things that people saw as a stamp of success. Being in my apartment, surrounded by shiny things, was a heavy reflection to witness. The glare of so much stuff slowly showed me that possessions are not the answer to fulfillment, and after working so hard to gain things that the world told me I should, I was met with another disappointment: this wasn't the answer.

I didn't stay in England. The emptiness was too heavy to bear. One day, I thought to myself, maybe it's just because my people aren't here in this country – if I want to see spiritualists, healers and yogis, I have to go to where those people are, and I certainly didn't see many around the town in which I was living.

On a whim I packed up my home and moved myself across the world to Sydney, Australia. There, I found myself in an overpriced, modern and lonely two-bedroom apartment overlooking the ocean. I didn't manage to enjoy this apartment too much because, by this point, I was just existing. I would spend most of my time in bed and only occasionally get up to do a reading or teach a class, then back to bed. I was scattered, disorganised and tired. I couldn't keep to a schedule. I let clients down. My business had grown too big for me to manage. This was a big sign that God wasn't in it because He always prepares us to keep the life we build with Him. But Satan doesn't. This is why we always lose what we build without Him.

Unless the LORD builds a house, the work of the builders is wasted. Unless the LORD protects a city, guarding it with sentries will do no good.

Psalms 127:1

I didn't have the skills to run a company at that time, being as spiritual as I was, and I was on a spiritual diet. This fluctuated from veganism to raw veganism. My iron was low. My body was frail. My skin was pale. The skin under my eyes was dark. My fingers were cold. My inspiration was lacking.

As 2019 wrapped up, whispers of an epidemic were around the corner. I didn't take this seriously as the fear mongering of the world had always been of zero interest to me. But what I did listen to, was a calling.

THE GRACE OF GOD

"Leave Sydney!" I kept hearing. Unsure why, I adhered to the call. The next weekend, I rented a car and drove eight hours up the east coast to the shores of Byron Bay. It was a popular place that I'd rarely visited, yet so many people had told me that I belonged there and not in Sydney. I spent the weekend with a friend and upon doing so, heard the call again. "Leave Sydney!" In the two days I was there, I decided to stay, despite my visa coming to an end in the next few weeks, having no home and no vehicle of my own. "Leave Sydney!"

My friend and I scrolled the internet for somewhere to live, but with every call I made I was told the same thing – bookings need to be two weeks in advance due to new mandatory regulations arising. Due to the spread of Covid-19, suddenly doors were closing. At 2pm, I called one last house. This time, rather than an estate agent answering, the landlord did – a kind man who offered to show me around the house in thirty minutes. My friend and I jumped in her car and made the ten-minute drive to a beautiful converted barn overlooking the shire. It was stunning. The doors opened up to a view of rolling hills and fields of banana trees. The kitchen and lounge were all open plan with windows as big as the house itself. The stairs led up to an open and spacious bedroom, filled with light and complete with beams where I'd one day hang plants. "I'll take it."

With the coming of dawn, the angels urged Lot, saying, "Hurry! Take your wife and your two daughters who are here, or you will be swept away when the city is punished." When he hesitated, the men grasped his hand and the hands of his wife and of his two daughters and led them safely out of the city, for the LORD was merciful to them. As soon as they had brought them out, one of them said, "Flee for your lives! Don't look back, and don't stop anywhere in the plain! Flee to the mountains or you will be swept away!"

> **But Lot said to them, "No, my lords, please! Your servant has found favour in your eyes, and you have shown great kindness to me in sparing my life. But I can't flee to the mountains; this disaster will overtake me, and I'll die. Look, here is a town near enough to run to, and it is small. Let me flee to it – it is very small, isn't it? Then my life will be spared." He said to him, "Very well, I will grant this request too; I will not overthrow the town you speak of. But flee there quickly, because I cannot do anything until you reach it."**
>
> *Genesis 19:15-16*

On the drive back to my friend's house, we stopped off at the local beach for a swim and giggled over the fact that I'd just signed a lease to a house in a country where I could not stay. Something, however, was on my side, even if I didn't know what.

Whilst at the beach, I reached for my phone and searched for courses in the area for which I could get a potential visa. I was met with the usual response at this time – closed due to Covid-19. No one was accepting new students and the students that were studying were being told not to come in.

However, I found a little course in a local town that taught Ayurvedic medicine, along with massage and healing therapies. I called, expecting nothing, but the phone was answered by the course leader – a brilliant man with an outstanding academic past, but one I shall keep private as it would be unladylike of me to reveal the secrets of others. He insisted on meeting me before accepting me on the course and, as I was leaving the next day, he agreed to meet me the morning of my drive back to Sydney. We spoke briefly about the course and he explained how and why he was able to stay open as this pandemic grew. He told me not to get the vaccination under any circumstances and that my vegan diet wouldn't be accepted here. "It is dry and damaging," he told me.

I agreed to meet his conditions and asked, before shaking his hand in agreement, if he'd like me to be in his class and if he was willing to teach me.

He nodded and we shook.

On the way home, I phoned my lawyer. A strong, Scottish woman who has saved me many times. She began to get my student visa under application. I then called my estate agent to tell them I wouldn't be renewing my lease. It was clear that they thought I was crazy due to there being talk of a lockdown but I insisted I was done. I drove the next eight hours with a smile. As I arrived home, my friend in Byron called.

"I've found a spiffing little car for you. It's for sale at the local garage."

I sent her the money and the car was mine. All I had to do now was pack up the few possessions I had, and rent a car to drive up. Within two weeks, I had moved. The first night I locked the door to my new home was the day we were told that we were all under lockdown.

I can honestly say, with hands on heart, that I never saw Covid-19. For the first year of it, I studied for my diploma, took swims in the ocean and went on long jungle walks with fellow students. I rarely wore a mask because Byron Bay didn't submit to government regulations and neither did those with whom I spent my time. Meanwhile, from the few I knew back in Sydney, I was informed of how terrible it was. Everyone wore masks and were locked in their apartments, leaving only for short walks or to get whatever food that was available.

However, I seemed protected. I never saw it and I never caught it. Whilst people saw brick walls, I saw green fields and whales jumping in front of the 5am sunrise. I received calls from my family back home, all in lockdown, allowed to leave their homes only once a day, yet I was totally protected. By the time Byron Bay was forced to submit to state regulations, I moved once again into the mountains of Tamworth, where I stayed for a few months before making my descent home to England in 2021. By the time I reached the UK, the pandemic was over, therefore I never saw Covid-19.

Into the Darkness

DARKNESS FALLS

However, it wasn't all roses and ribbons during this time, for whilst I was in the midst of it all, I met a man. He was fun and spontaneous. He was childlike. He was free-spirited. But he also wasn't responsible, mature, authoritative, or ambitious. I found myself in an eighteen-month relationship with a man who was too afraid to chase his dreams. He was too afraid to work for something, and too afraid to make something of himself, despite the fact that he was brilliant. He had a brilliant mind, vast like mine, and a heart that had depth. I sacrificed every piece of me to give him the confidence that I believed he deserved, and in that eighteen months I learned some things. I learnt how to be a breadwinner. I learnt how to take care of another person financially. I learnt how to cook and how to encourage someone. But, eventually, I just couldn't look at myself in the mirror. My longing to understand who I was and why I was here made the emptiness press against my chest. I had moved so many times and the emptiness had met me in every home I created, so maybe that wasn't the answer. Maybe, it was my relationship. I needed to feel secure and wanted, so we made the decision to marry and move to the state where he was raised.

The night of my wedding, we conceived; but when I told him that I was pregnant, he was most displeased. He knew that we both weren't responsible enough to create a family. But really, he was afraid to have that commitment.

We both knew that things weren't right. We both knew that we were on different pages. But neither of us could walk away in a mature manner. When I was six weeks pregnant, we found ourselves in a disagreement and, rather than coming to conflict resolution, his response was that he was done. He asked me to pack my suitcases and leave.

I obliged and filled my two suitcases with anything I could find. I had given up my life for him, so the fear of where I'd go and what would happen to me was prevalent. He dedicated his day to driving me eight hours back to Byron Bay where he'd met me, and he dropped me off in a small room that I had booked on that eight hour drive. He kissed me on the forehead and he looked me in the eye and said, "You'll be fine. You're the strongest woman I know." He turned on his heels and left.

The emptiness and loneliness that followed was the least of my problems. I was at a crossroad with about twelve different options, neither one I wanted to take. Two weeks later, leaving the decision to the last minute, I decided to abort the pregnancy. The day I went into labour, there were no spirit guides to comfort me. The pain was unbearable and, as I was laying on the bathroom floor, clenching the glass shower door with my little fingers, begging for mercy and begging any of my spirit guides to relieve the pain, no one came. Satan had me right where he wanted me: alone. I had spent the last six years in an industry where my life resided around speaking to spirit guides and angels, and having a close relationship with them, but the moment I needed them the most, no one was there. I was met only with my perpetual loneliness.

That emptiness filled the room. I managed to fall asleep around 8pm, then found my body waking up in the early hours, covered in blood. On the surface, I was in pain; but in the supernatural, I had made a blood sacrifice to the enemy. I didn't know it then, but life would never be the same again.

Shortly after this experience, anger become my friend. The only thing I could take real responsibility for was letting this happen. I took responsibility for not reading the signs properly and I took responsibility for over-giving and oversharing. I took responsibility for being a victim of my life instead of the owner of my life. Still, the anger persisted; and one night I felt this voice move through me. Looking back, I knew it wasn't mine, but at the time I surely felt it was. My abortion had let in the darkest demons. They hated me and I hated people. I became just like them and I sought out power. I returned to the power of being a witch, because maybe I really was one. Maybe I really was that powerful, I just wasn't standing in my power. Maybe I needed to. This was a feeling I held onto for safety. If I didn't hold onto it, I'd surely drown, and so I clung onto it all the way home back to England, where I would begin my life in witchcraft.

FACE TO FACE WITH THE DEVIL

Going through an abortion opened so many doors to an evil world. I was knocked off my feet pretty fast and, what I thought was the power I was seeking, was in fact me following a dark and powerless path.

I invested in a cauldron. I invested in candles. I began selling oils for healing. I began performing weekly rituals. I began doing spell work for clients. The spells all worked, but the sacrifice it took to manipulate energy like that was not energy that I really had in me. My body felt different. I gained thirty pounds. I ate for comfort and found myself in gluttony, and although I found myself in a beautiful cottage in the middle of the Cotswolds, the emptiness was waiting for me.

One night, after living there for just a few months, I awoke to a cold room. Not physically cold, spiritually cold. I can only describe it as a room without God. The sheep in the field next to me were bleating under a full moon, adding a sense of eeriness to the darkness. Something was in that room with me. It wasn't unusual to see things, for I'd seen things all my life, but whatever was in my room that time was new.

In the left corner of the room, a tall, dark figure appeared. I knew it wasn't an angel because the angelic beings I'd seen previously always entered the room by telling me first to not be afraid. As it came closer to my face, the figure of a goat formed itself. Its body, however, was human. Sort of.

It approached my bed, where I was laying on my back, paralysed with fear. It reached out and placed its hands on my knees and sought to climb on top of me. I refused and pulled away. It stopped and stared at me in a way that began to manipulate my emotions. I suddenly found myself having compassion for this beast in front of me. Maybe he was misunderstood, just like me, I thought. The more I softened to it, the more I let it in. This is how we open doors to evil. We say 'yes' to it.

After this encounter, I found myself seeking more answers and dived into the occult. I wanted to know more and more. I wanted to know how this realm worked in people's lives. But, the more I studied it, the more doors I opened and the more demons stepped in.

Before I knew it, I was waking up to the smell of smoke and flames often. Panicked, thinking I had left the oven on, I'd run downstairs only to find nothing and instead to find the smell completely gone. Looking back, I know that on that night, I smelt Hell. It smelt like burning flesh, flames and sodium. Whatever was plaguing me at night, surely came from the pits of Hell, but I didn't know about demons. I didn't know about darkness in that way. I was a New Ager. I was a hippie. Surely there's no such thing as evil. That doesn't exist in our world, I thought.

However, I was coming face to face with it on a daily basis. For two weeks I didn't sleep, because every time I tried to sleep it would try to get into my body. This was a disgusting feeling. I felt powerless. Luckily for me, I knew a fellow witch. She was a strong woman who was a powerful deliverance minister. God sent her to my rescue, and removed the demon from my house. I felt so powerless. I couldn't keep hiring someone and paying someone to remove demons if they showed up. I had to find authority and be able to do this myself. So, for the next year, I found myself experimenting and exploring the world of demons, though I honestly thought I was playing with ghosts. Demons often disguise themselves as past loved ones and lost children, all of which flocked to me because the door was well open. Little did I notice at the time, but Jesus was calling me home.

I remember looking at my altar in my office, where I actually had a statue of the devil. I had a statue of Lucifer. I also had statues of Hecate, Kali Ma, all kinds of deities. One day I then simply thought to myself, well, I may as well get a little crucifix in here as I have everything else – I may as well have Jesus too, thinking naively that He was simply a prophet, just the same as Buddha and Krishna. But before I was able to purchase anything of the sort, I found myself on the move once again. The emptiness had gotten the better of me. My life felt chaotic. I was tired. I didn't have to work as much as I used to because I was selling my courses. This meant that I didn't have to sell my time for money anymore. It meant that I could write a book I had been meaning to write. It meant that I could be with friends. It meant that I could explore the world. But no matter where I drove to or who I spent time with, the emptiness would always call my name.

But this time, peace was also knocking.

Something in me called me to simplify my life and sell everything. I wanted to live a quiet life. I made a decision right there and then to head back to Australia, as I had unfinished business there. I'd left in such a hurry and, being back in England for two years, I missed the sun. I missed the palm trees. I missed the way of life and figured I had nothing to lose. I'd spent two years in torment, trying to heal the wounds of having an abortion and the guilt that comes with it, along with the disgust that I had for myself, the missing of my child, all of this was catching up to me. I needed a simple life.

THE WAY, THE TRUTH AND THE LIFE

I headed back to Australia and found a small humble apartment with a tiny kitchenette, living room, bedroom and bathroom. This was all I needed. I had a yoga studio down the road that I could walk to and I even signed up for yoga training. Before I knew it, I was once again surrounded by yogis and philosophers. These women held breathwork retreats and healing circles. They ran free through the beaches at night and danced under the moon. I thought that maybe these were my people and maybe, just maybe, I'll finally find peace.

Every morning, I'd awake before the sunrise, throw a beach dress over a bikini, step out of my apartment, and glide down the steps until I was on the beach. From there, I'd walk for miles with my book held out in front of me. I'm sure it looked strange to passersby, but my heart was desperate to be filled with lady wisdom. I read and I read.

One morning, I decided to take my book on a walk to my favourite cove. I went here often as it lacked a crowd and I've never been a fan of those. I'd much rather be alone. When I arrived, I looked out at the clear water and surrounding rocks and, just as the sun began to rise, I drove in. The cool water always soothed my skin and I often let my long hair cascade and drip down my back until it dried in the heat. I climbed out and found a little resting spot overlooking the water. I settled in and let the sun begin to warm my skin and, as it did, I felt a warm rush of love penetrate throughout my whole body.

At first, I gave credit to nature. Who doesn't feel better living in nature like this?

But, soon, it happened again. What was that? I'd not felt a feeling of love like that before. As I bathed in it, my attention began to be pulled upon as the presence of someone appeared to my left. As I looked over, there sat next to me, was Jesus. His white robe was loosely hung from His body and His hair was long enough to touch His shoulders, but the part of Him that shone the most was His smile and the warmth in His eyes. I could write poetry all day long about just His eyes. I could tell that they could move mountains, even in my state of shock.

My curiosity peaked. I asked Him why He was here.

He said nothing.

I asked Him if He was here to help me.

He said nothing.

I blamed myself for not getting any answers because, in my mind and in my New Age beliefs, Jesus was a Master and you have to be a Master yourself to be able to connect with Him. Maybe I had to work on myself more.

I couldn't sit in His presence for long. I didn't know it at the time but His presence was so powerful that it may have destroyed me to sit with Him for more than a minute or so. The demons in me trembled with fear and wanted to run, but of course I knew nothing of the sort at the time. We sat there together for what felt like eternity, but in actual fact it was two minutes. Then, with my book in hand, I strolled home, pondering on the encounter. I had no idea what it had meant and why it had happened, but something in me felt different. And so it was.

I carried on with life as I always had. I took my morning strolls with my New Age books, spent time with friends having philosophical conversations, and pulled myself through my yoga training. I was living the heightened hippie life, minus the drugs. However, something started to creep in: the truth.

One morning, a flock of friends and I gathered at a local coffee shop. Out the front was a little wooden stage layered with rugs and cushions where the barefooted gathered. We clumped together with legs crossed in a small clump and surrounded ourselves with the usual concoctions of coffee, spicy cardamom cacao shots and slices of banana bread adorned in little petals. As I listened to the conversation that went around the circle, I noticed that the inspiration just wasn't hitting that day. Instead, I was confused. The women around me were discussing healing festivals that they had recently attended and, instead of feeling intrigued about the whole thing, I actually felt disgusted. Why would one want to go to such an event?

As I walked home that day I felt conflicted, though I didn't understand why. I decided to hash it out over a voice note with a friend everyone called the Duchess, as she had recently been feeling something similar. We both circled this concept of so-called healing. If it really worked, why do we have to keep going to such events? It no longer made sense.

"I think," she told me, "that in order to be truly healed, we need… God."

It was a surprise to hear her say that, and yet it didn't surprise me as much as it should.

As the following months rolled on, I was offered opportunities that every New Ager dreams of being offered. I was hosting retreats in various locations around Australia, and now had three booked, including the ultimate one in Bali, Indonesia.

That March, I found myself planted amongst fifteen women who had journeyed into the wilderness for a yoga and breathwork retreat hosted by myself and two other experts. On the second day, everyone gathered on their yoga mats and laid themselves down under the music of my friend's singing. Under the sound of her voice, they all began to slip into an emotional coma, then all begin to cry. Their bodies twisted and distorted as they revelled in their emotions for an hour. My friend walked amongst the bodies and offered hugs to some and a gentle touch on the shoulder to others as they weep for their lives. One woman remained on the floor for an hour after the ceremony in shock, rocking back and forth while being held by one of the other hosts. I looked around the room at what had just happened. Although I'd normally see it as a mighty success – for I had long believed that indulging in emotions such as these was healing – that day I saw something very different. To describe it, I used a word that I'd never even used before: demonic.

A few days later, I found myself back at home, standing in front of my bathroom mirror, braiding my long, sun-kissed hair. As I did so, I stopped in my tracks as I had a revelation: since my encounter with Jesus I had not read my books, I had not gone to any healing circles, and I had any conversations about such things.

As I was struck with this revelation, I picked up my phone to share it with the Duchess. She had had the same revelation a few months before me, as she had also had an encounter with God that had shattered the illusion of her world too. We both sat in silence under the realisation that Jesus is the only one who heals and, when He does, it is done. There is no need to go back for more, for it's written and it's complete. Jesus saves and Jesus heals. Without Him, we live only in an illusion of healing and the illusion causes us to go back for more, or to simply 'top up'.

The Inverted World

EXPOSING SATAN'S KINGDOM

So many people believe in Satanism, though claim they don't believe in Satan or in Hell. This seems a little strange to me, for it is like believing in the home that stands around you but not believing that anyone built it. This is deathly common and the reason behind it is because Satan hides. He has so many masks that, whilst you may be accusing a fellow man of worshipping the devil, you can be doing the same.

The scripture tells us that our Heavenly father created angelic beings. Amongst them were three Archangels: Michael, the Archangel of warfare; Gabrielle, the Archangel of messages; and Lucifer, the Archangel of worship. Over time, Lucifer began to look upon the Lord and desire to not just be like Him, but to be better. He told the angels in heaven that He would one day be better. Some believed him, whilst others didn't. However, as pride began to engulf him, he fell from the heavens like lightning because darkness cannot exist with the light of heaven.

You *were* the seal of perfection, Full of wisdom and perfect in beauty. You were in Eden, the garden of God; Every precious stone *was* your covering: The sardius, topaz, and diamond, Beryl, onyx, and jasper, Sapphire, turquoise, and emerald with gold. The workmanship of your timbrels and pipes was prepared for you on the day you were created.

You *were* the anointed cherub who covers; I established you; You were on the holy mountain of God; You walked back and forth in the midst of fiery stones. You *were* perfect in your ways from the day you were created, till iniquity was found in you.

By the abundance of your trading, you became filled with violence within, And you sinned; Therefore I cast you as a profane thing out of the mountain of God; and I destroyed you, O covering cherub, From the midst of the fiery stones.

Your heart was lifted up because of your beauty; you corrupted your wisdom for the sake of your splendour; I cast you to the ground, I laid you before kings, that they might gaze at you.

You defiled your sanctuaries by the multitude of your iniquities, by the iniquity of your trading; therefore I brought fire from your midst; it devoured you, and I turned you to ashes upon the earth in the sight of all who saw you.

All who knew you among the peoples are astonished at you; you have become a horror and *shall be* no more forever.

The seventy-two returned with joy and said, "Lord, even the demons submit to us in your name." He replied, "I saw Satan fall like lightning from heaven. I have given you authority to trample on snakes and scorpions and to overcome all the power of the enemy; nothing will harm you. However, do not rejoice that the spirits submit to you, but rejoice that your names are written in heaven.

Luke 10:17-20

As much as my life was now changing, I was on fire for the Lord and that fire hated Satan. I intended to be a threat to him and that he should be afraid, for I now knew who I was, how much my Heavenly Father loved, and I had direct access to Him and all He wanted me to do. I'm obedient and I'm loyal. Satan should be scared.

I saw him as he really was and how he really acts. He loathes you and all the fruits you attempt to bear. He is waiting behind every corner ready to lie, steal and cheat. His demons are the faces to whom you speak, thinking it's your lost Grandmother or late husband. He's the one whose fingers move through the tarot cards and it's his familiar spirits who watch you like a hawk, ready to give you a prediction through a psychic medium as to what your recent whereabouts are, so that you can sit there in amazement that someone knows something that no one else knows. He tells you that it's your job to heal your ancestors and places this upon your shoulders. He releases dopamine hits every time you experience the inverted healing, in the hope that you'll never experience the real healing of Jesus Christ, and he waits patiently for that dopamine to leave, then prepares you to find the next healing release, hoping you'll never discover true salvation. He makes you think you're righteous for seeking such a life, and shakes in his kingdom in fear of you discovering your true birthright and real father.

As long as you live this life, you are no threat to him, for you know not who you are or from where you came. Not only do you not know of your kingdom, you can't even see the pearly gate upon which to enter and, if you were to ever begin to unravel the truth, he's waiting to feed you another lie.

After these realisations, my old world began to crumble in front of me. Yet Satan still wanted me! He'd had me for this long, and not only did he not want to lose me, He knew that the work I'd do in the kingdom of God would be to expel many of his demons, for I was a woman on fire for Jesus. Suddenly, all the dreams I once had were being handed to me: trips to Bali, yoga certificates, and a new book were all dangled in front of me. Satan was trying to tempt me with all the shiny things.

But nothing could compare to the glow of the heart of Christ. I was done.

I plucked up my courage and made a call to my friend (and Bali co-host) to tell her that I could no longer go to Bali. We'd already booked several women into the retreat, so it came as a disappointment to her.

"What do we do with the women who have already booked?" she asked in a panic.

"Refund them. I don't want their money," I responded and I meant it.

I spent the next month refunding those who had made a booking to walk with me privately, and any new clients who wanted to book were refused on the spot.

So of course the enemy attacked again. I went viral.

One measly reel went out on a Wednesday morning. I thought nothing of it as I clicked the button to post it. But by that afternoon, my phone was consistently flashing. That reel ended up receiving a million views in just three days, and my following went from three thousand to one hundred thousand in those three days. I woke to hundreds of messages every morning and, suddenly, everyone wanted to work with me, interview me, meet me, even marry me.

But as time went by, I could see that this was Satan's blessing, and it's so easy to spot when you know what it looks like. Satan's blessings look shiny on the outside, but they're a hollow shell on the inside. Having hundreds of thousands of followers brought me no new clients or any genuine value. The clients I had previously, who were curious about my new ways of thinking, got pushed out by the clobber of followers that I now had. My client list was completely infiltrated, so although people would find my work and see a large following, it was just a shiny case of nothingness as Satan's offers always are. The world is filled with people who think that going viral will bring them fulfillment, but they'll be met with a lie if it's sent from Satan, because all he has to offer is a whole load of nothingness wrapped in shiny paper. It is and ever will compare to our Father in Heaven and the blessings that come from Him, for His are everlasting.

YOU ARE NOT GOD

Just like Satan, the New Age believe that they're God, that they can manifest all they want and need (but you rarely see this) and that they are the creator of their own reality. As I look back upon this time of my life, it makes me feel quite unpleasant to think that I once believed that I was essentially God or that I could do as he does.

The more I dabbled, the more depressed I got, but you wouldn't ever hear me say this. How can we spend hours a week reliving our past pain and dissecting our pain without our actual world becoming painful? The more we dig, the more we find, and the more we find, the more we become. That industry led me into disliking everyone around me and filled me with pride. I thought I was often right, but now I sought not to be right, but instead to bow down, no matter who was in front of me.

I have watched so many families become disconnected the moment a woman in the family begins to seek tarot readers, fortune tellers, astrologists and all of the sort, because Satan continues to go after the woman and her emotions, as he did with Eve. He still tries to make women in marriages think there's someone better out there for them and turns wives away from their husbands. He still sells you what he has, but has to first make you think that you don't have it. He turns daughters against mothers and mothers against husbands. But for me enough was enough. The blood of Christ was now on my family and I moved knowing that the name of Jesus on my family would scare away any demonic influence in the future, for He doesn't just deliver us, we also deliver those around us in due time.

What a relief to know that I'm not God! Therefore, and forever, I now bow myself to Him and to His name, for His will be done, not mine. One of the selfish habits I had been taught in New Age spirituality was that the world revolved around me. It taught me that I could manifest things and that I had the power to create my own world. Over the years, Satan had me following breadcrumbs as I 'manifested' a new friend or a few extra pounds in my bank. How sad to look back and to think that this was abundance. Thinking that the universe was God instead of what God created, and thinking that it had power to move my life in the direction of what I wanted. My words said I was happy (and I really believed I was) but deep down, I was tired. So many spiritual people are. This is because they have been told that they're God (or a form of God) and that they're in control of their destiny. How exhausting. Putting ourselves in His shoes is draining beyond belief. Spirituality is filled with tired people, but they are yet to stop and really ponder as to why.

The industry is filled with single women and men seeking pleasure and dopamine. They look for it in each other, in a healing modality or in a plant medicine. They call upon their dead ancestors and seek wisdom, yet find only Satan's, which means it soon collapses and they're back to their everyday life of seeking more. The whole industry is empty and glutinous.

If we're all the creator of our own reality, then why don't we all have our dream life? If we do get a glimpse of our dream, then why do we have to try so hard to keep it. Satan entangles his musical notes all throughout a spiritual world without God and leaves his victims drained, chasing little things that people think are so wonderful, yet God has an entire life planned for them, which has blessings beyond the comprehension of most spiritual people. Satan sends breadcrumbs and laughs as we follow them. He sends his children out to mimic spirits and ghosts, making us think that we're talking to our past loved ones, when really we're speaking to demons in disguise.

They're always watching us. They're everywhere. They stalk your every move to plot against you. They never want you to discover your purpose in life nor do they want you to know your Heavenly Father, as it would bring you into the birthright of the kingdom of God. Yet so many people would tell me that they know there's more to life, yet they can't access it. Many think that they have discovered a secret to the universe when they discover New Age practises, but they've only found the doop. They found Satan's replica.

The result of going down this path is destruction. It leads to loss of relationships, divided families, a financial yoyo, a consistent longing, and a mindset that eventually becomes self-indulgent. Everyone is out for themselves and searches for those who serve them, instead of who they can serve. Satan prows of the kind-hearted and the tender loving. God's children, who are here to bring the love of the Holy Spirit to all they meet, now run in Satan's circles, chasing the extra bit of money or friend who he's sent into their life and calling it a blessed manifestation.

The Lord humbled me from this life and I am forever grateful. After a three-day fast, I found myself bowing on my knees to the God I follow and getting quite the wake-up call. Being delivered from the sin of pride is an extremely painful experience and my Heavenly Father lead me into it so gently as not to cause harm. After three days of hunger, I began to witness myself in my pride and the Lord showed me all those I'd hurt because of it. He showed me what pride had done, not just in regard to pushing me away from Him, but to the path of destruction it had led me down. Due to years of 'healing', I had pushed away all those who loved me. Healing, when done through therapy, psychology, regression or any of these types of forms, is truly damaging for it asks you to put a microscope to the painful experiences you may have gone through. But just as Satan always does, he has taken a truth from God and lied about the rest.

To acknowledge a painful experience that we went through is the one truth. The remaining truth, and all we have left to do, is pray to our Heavenly Father and ask Him to lift it off our shoulders. So many times I have knelt down and cried to Him and asked Him to do such a thing. Within every new moment I now feel the weight lifted off of my shoulders, and as my tears dissipate so does the painful story. Never to relive it again and never to allow Satan to use it against me. This is not what the New Age does. What it does is to ask you to relive it multiple times, or it makes you think that you can heal it by seeing it and sending a spectrum of love and light on it. This may make someone feel better for a moment, but now the cycle begins. "Now I want to see what else I need to heal," I would say. But it would only start a cycle of being addicted to my emotions and addicted to the euphoria of a healing session.

Our Heavenly Father never asks us to seek pain. Why would he? He doesn't want us to relive the past and certainly doesn't wish to see us hurting. Would you like to see your child hurting on a regular basis?

To point this out to a New Ager is tricky, for they will all tell you the same thing. They will tell you that it's helping them, and their life has changed and gotten better since. This is partly true because the ego pats them on the back for showing up for themselves, but Satan still laughs at you. Of course, it's difficult to know a life without this form of healing, but once you know God and see the real way to live, you can leave your hamster wheel of healing and live beyond this. You'll laugh at yourself too.

DOWNWARD FACING DEVIL

How I didn't clock on to what yoga really is, seems beyond me now. All I can put it down to is that we're all under a spell, never really seeing the truth that's right in front of us. I remember a Christian woman once telling me that she didn't do yoga because, in her words, it was demonic, and at the time I thought she was being ridiculous and dramatic. However, I was wrong and she was right.

When I had my first encounter with Jesus, I was still doing my yoga teacher training. But now, when I attended my weekly yoga session, my eyes were fully open. As I assembled my body into a pose that supposedly mimicked something like Kali Ma, the goddess of destruction, I suppose that once upon a time, when a yoga teacher told me that I was yoking with a goddess, I thought I was powerful. If I had the power of destruction then nothing and no one could hurt me. Yet, they still did, and I still hurt them. In each yoga hour, I merely yoked myself to death scenes (warrior sequences) and so many demons, no wonder I lost my identity.

After I began to see clearly, I asked a fellow yogi friend why she felt she needed to do yoga every couple of days. Her answer was the same as all the others I asked – to stay ahead of her emotions and to bring her peace. It became obvious to me that anything that calls us to do repeatedly seems to be a lie. If we must go back to seek more peace, did we ever truly have it? Peace does not come and go. Once it is truly felt, it stays.

One day, as I was standing in my bathroom in front of my mirror, it hit me. I'd been saved. I'd been healed. Ever since Jesus came to me that day, my whole life had become different. His presence pushed me out of my old life and into His. He'd healed me. I had gone from living out a career in healing for over eight years to not thinking anything about such a thing. So I stood there, feet cold on the bathroom floor, and I didn't move. I realised that my entire New Age belief system that we have to heal was a cat and mouse chase we could never win, and we never win it because we cannot heal ourselves and we cannot heal each other. Jesus heals.

This revelation swept through my body so fast I didn't know if I was warm or cold. My amazement was followed by total and absolute gratitude – that I was being given the opportunity to be born again and to do what I was actually here to do. I could see the fabrics of how the enemy works and how he takes God's story for you and his purpose, inverts it and puts you into a torturous loop. I was in that loop for eight years and, although the beginning of my work in the New Age looks exciting as I look back on it, I became more lost than ever as the years go on.

So many clients have told me the same thing. They tell me that the beginning stages of their self-healing journey was profound. But as the years clocked on, they only became more confused than ever and even felt more broken. But how could this be if they were healing?

It was because they *weren't* healing. They were having dopamine hits after ceremonies and the ego around their trauma was being fed, which meant they slowly became more self-righteous and more self-obsessed. Thinking back, I see that if a healing ceremony worked, why go back for another?

The whole industry was a lie and it got ripped from under my feet that day. I saw all the cracks and I saw the doorway to the demonic.

The advice that each individual usually received whilst on a psychedelic trip was only advice that would lead to suffering. It came wrapped in a bow, but when such guidance was followed, the person would end up worse off in the end. The whole world was infiltrated and nothing I did could stop me from seeing it. I didn't want to stop seeing it. I wanted to be shown it all, and so I was.

The whole of 2024 was a rebirth for me. I thought differently, ate differently, dressed differently and moved differently. I no longer fit into my old life, and I did feel alone at times, but God was always calling upon me and I tried my best to listen, whilst also watching my whole life change. I couldn't listen to anyone use blasphemous language anymore. Not even on the TV. I couldn't stand to hear people talk about their new self-love rituals and I certainly didn't want to hear anymore self-obsessed stories from any New Agers.

By May of 2024, only four months after I had had my encounter with Jesus, I claimed the title of a Christian woman and I've never looked back.

There was such a difference in me now that I could see, and as I looked in the mirror brushing my hair that morning, I froze as I realised that the emptiness was no longer there. It was gone. I searched for it for a moment. I closed my eyes and felt my heart. Nothing.

I wandered over to my bed and sat down puzzled. I looked around the room, thinking, and my eyes shifted everywhere.

Where was my emptiness? It was like having a long-lost friend. I'd carried it for thirty-four years. Suddenly he was gone. I didn't understand. I thought to myself, when did I last feel it? Like a person looking for their lost car keys? I racked my brain. When did I last feel it? What did it feel like? And then it dawned on me. I hadn't felt it since I had encountered Jesus Christ, and in that moment I realised that He was the ultimate and only healer.

But he was pierced for our transgressions, he was crushed for our iniquities; the punishment that brought us peace was on him, and by his wounds we are healed.

Isaiah 53:5

To be Sealed

THE FLESHY HEART

Upon returning home to a blossoming England, I found a small place to stay and leant on the support of a great friend to get myself settled. Twenty minutes down the road from my town was another. It was titled 'England's most beautiful town' in the Cotswolds, and there I found the church. I was nervous about going because I'd yet to really have any experience in church life. It seemed so daunting. I didn't know what to wear, where to sit or even if I should sit, but my Heavenly Father was my chaperone. I ended up visiting the church one Wednesday afternoon and simply wandered around the building for a while. I was starstruck by the artwork that filled the walls and old bibles laid out on display. As I ran my fingers over them, I stopped at one that was open.

There shall not be found among you *any one* that maketh his son or his daughter to pass through the fire, *or* that useth divination, *or* an observer of times, or an enchanter, or a witch, or a charmer, or a consulter with familiar spirits, or a wizard, or a necromancer. For all that do these things *are* an abomination unto the Lord: and because of these

abominations the Lord thy God doth drive them out from before thee.
Deuteronomy 18:9-12

I was convicted. I stood in this wide-open church, staring at this text in shock. I'd read it before but now, in the house of the Lord, it was staring right back at me. Shame sank into my heart and, as I continued my walk of the church, I found myself standing underneath a large, golden painting of Jesus on the cross. I stood underneath it with my head down, ashamed. My mind flashed back to all the things that I'd taken part in, and my friends and family too. Witchcraft seemed to be in my bloodline and it all seemed so normal then; but now, so abnormal.

I wandered out of the church to the office building next door, where I was greeted by a woman with a smile that I didn't feel I deserved. We got chatting and I told her that I was looking for a church to attend. She was thrilled. I could feel the love of Christ in her heart and the peace in her mannerisms. Over the next thirty minutes, we chatted about the church and what to expect from the weekly services, including Holy Communion. I didn't know much about this but my heart wanted it. I wanted Him. I wanted to know Him and I wanted to live for Him. He was the reason I was even here. My nerves fluttered with anticipation of a world of just Him and I, as I knew that this was the intimacy I'd been looking for my whole life.

When she discovered I was nervous about attending a service, she put me at ease. "Why don't I meet you here on Sunday about fifteen minutes before the service and we can sit together?" she said with a smile.

This was when I first observed God's grace. He was shepherding me into His home.

I attended a couple of services before I took holy Communion. On that day, I walked to the front of the church and was greeted by a tall man holding a plate of bread. He prayed over me and I bowed my head as I picked a piece of the bread off of the tray. I then stepped to one side to greet the other man who was holding a large silver chalice with engravings all up its sides. I took a sip and bowed once again. I returned to my seat, still clutching my little piece of bread except, it wasn't bread. It was Him. It was His body, right there, in my little hand. My heart swelled and I felt the urge to run to a dark corner of the church to weep but I remained still. I bowed my head in the chair and ate it in silence.

I was invited to spend time with the other church members after the service, but I declined. I had to go back to my car to release the fountain of tears that was building up in me. My heart felt like it had turned soft in that instant and I cried the entire drive home. My whole body had become so sensitive that I barely knew what to do when I returned home except read my bible and sit in silence.

That night, I was introduced to a song. I never really listened to gospel music before, but at a friend's insistence, I played a recommendation and I was flawed. I found myself weeping once again. My heart was open like a floodgate and I couldn't switch it off. I was in love with Jesus. He was in my heart and He was becoming my heart.

A new heart also will I give you, and a new spirit will I put within you: and I will take away the stony heart out of your flesh, and I will give you a heart of flesh.

Ezekiel 36:26

THE SEAL OF GOD

That night, I flopped down on my bed with emotional exhaustion for it was the day that my heart grew seven times bigger. But it wasn't over. As I prepared for sleep, I felt the presence of someone in the room with me. It felt familiar, like rediscovering an old perfume from times gone by. I knew it the second it entered. It was Him.

I opened my eyes and there He was. Being in the magnificence of such glory won't be something I'll ever be able to convey with worldly words, but there He was, standing at the foot of my bed. I felt my heart break immediately as I was a witness to a crown made of thorns that pushed against His bleeding skin. His robes were torn and dishevelled, but His eyes were not of this world. My heart broke on the spot and as He walked closer to me I felt myself resisting Him as His presence pushed up against my sin.

He looked down at me and said, "I'm going to wash your feet."

I immediately pushed my hands up at Him to say 'no' as my eyes filled with tears. I didn't deserve to be served by the living saviour.

He said nothing but processed to place His hands on my feet. His touch was gentle yet it was painful. I couldn't fully comprehend what was happening but every cell within my flesh was resisting His touch.

He walked around to the side of the bed that I lay on and, with a few words and one simple gesture, He told me to put my hands by my side with my palms up; I obeyed. He raised His left hand to expose a large wound in the centre that appeared to still be bleeding, and reached over to place it palm to palm with my right. He did the same with the other hand. As I lay there with Him resting on my hands, I watched his blood pour onto my skin. He moved both hands up my arms, leaving a trail of blood up my lily-white arms and placed them on my chest, leaving bloody handprints around my collar bones and my heart. He lifted both hands and placed them on my face, holding me in an embrace. He looked me in the eyes like a lost child whom He was so overjoyed to have found. He placed one hand on my forehead, leaving a bloody handprint, then placed them on my womb and down my legs to my feet. He remained at the foot of the bed for quite some time as I lay there, overwhelmed.

My body was shaking and my hands felt like I was holding lead balloons. I wanted to ask why but I didn't feel worthy to ask any questions. My voice trembling, I asked for permission to ask a question, to which He gave one gracious head bow with a smile that came from His eyes, not His mouth.

"Why are my hands so heavy?" I asked.

His response was, "that is the heaviness of the cross."

It felt like a small lightning bolt had moved up my spine as He spoke, causing all my sweat glands to open and a small furnace rushed throughout my body. He remained at my feet for a while longer, then reached down to hold up a large, golden embroidered book. It looked like it had been carved out of a block of gold from the Earth. He opened it and held it up in front of me. I attempted to dry my eyes and focus on the words of the page but I struggled. He gestured to come closer.

As I did, I saw my name: Laura Ansell. I looked up at Him, puzzled. "That's me," I said. "You know me? You know my name?"

Another wave of undeserved-ness washed over my body. It felt like the blood in my body was going through a transmogrification and it hurt.

"You are mine," He said, His eyes again smiling.

The weight of my hands laid me down once again and I wept.

He walked back to the side of my bed once again and, as I gazed upon Him, He shifted right in front of my eyes. He was no longer Jesus on the cross. He was now Jesus, the Messiah. The son of God. The living God. His glory lit up the whole room. Who needs a side light when you have Christ? His blood disappeared and instead He glowed with a golden oil. He lifted His left hand as if to tell me that we were going to do this again.

I placed both hands by my sides with my palms up and tried my best to keep still even though I felt my own blood vibrating.

He placed His hands on mine and I watched the most beautiful golden oil seep from His hands to mine. He ran the golden oil up my arms and placed them once again on my heart. He then cupped my face with His hands and gazed into my eyes. He kept His gaze as He took His left hand and drew a cross with the golden oil on my forehead. He then placed His hands on my womb and remained there.

I knew I was forgiven. My blood vibrated so intensely that I began to feel my body shake like I'd been out in the cold all day.

He ran the oil down my legs and to my feet. He remained there for a brief moment, then He disappeared.

They were told not to harm the grass of the Earth or any green plant or any tree, but only those people who do not have the seal of God on their foreheads.

Revelation 9:4

CHOSEN AT LAST

As a child, I saw the best in everyone. I recognised a big heart when I saw one, but as I grew into an adult and began to offer this love to men, I couldn't find a single one who would receive it. It felt almost like the love I had for people repelled them, and this encounter expanded on that for I certainly couldn't receive the love that Jesus was offering me.

Some have felt my love to be too much for them, whilst others have felt undeserving of it. Some have run away when I got close, and others have created arguments in an attempt to make my heart smaller and easier to be around. Men have wanted to rent me but not own me. They have wanted me in their life but didn't want to claim me as theirs. They have wanted a piece of me but didn't want me to be their responsibility. No matter what man I gave my heart to, they used it to fill themselves up, then discarded me like a piece of paper. It pushed against their emotional traumas and own undeserving-ness and every time I'd get pushed out.

I wept and wailed for days on end. "God," I said, "no man ever chooses me."

I laid down for just a moment to let the beat of my broken heart catch its rhythm and, as I did, I felt the warmth of His arms embracing me. His presence enveloped all around me and the sheer focus that He had on the tears that fell from my big, blue eyes was overwhelming.

As I rested in His arms, He spoke to me. "I choose you. I made you. You are mine."

This was the day I realised that the enemy had lied. I was lovable and I was worth choosing, for my Father had chosen me all along. He never abandoned me. He let me make mistakes over and over again and remained patient. He watched me stray from Him so many times but never turned His back on me as I did Him. The image of how much He loved me made me fall deep into repentance.

Dear Heavenly Father,

I'm so sorry. I'm so sorry that I abandoned you when you never abandoned me. I'm so sorry that I thought a man could love me the way that you love me and I'm so sorry that I held them to a standard that only you can keep. I'm sorry if this caused them to feel as if they could never be enough. I'm sorry if this harmed their self-esteem. I didn't know.

Heavenly Father, I'm so sorry. Please forgive me and show me mercy. I pray, in the name of Jesus, that you show me a better way and that you show me how I can love you with no walls, only purity. Show me my childlike love for you, Father. Unveil me in your arms and restore me in your image. I pray this in Jesus name,

Amen.

The only man who ever accepted all the love I had to offer was Him and, when He received it, the feeling of relief was finally found. It's so lonely for us to wander the world with a big heart. Most people are afraid and guarded. Many want lust instead of love. They want to love you but only at a distance. They love the idea of you but not the real you. Once I realised that I could pour my love into Him, life felt full. It also allowed me to reach a deep understanding for the women I saw who went from relationship to relationship, desperate to feel loved by any man who would have them. Their desperation deceived them because it delighted the enemy so much: to see God's daughter give her heart and her body to a man who had not earned her. I'm sure he enjoyed watching these women settle for men who didn't show them off, who didn't claim them, who gawked at other women and lusted over naked flesh on the internet. He deceives these women so much that so many of them think this is either normal or acceptable.

My Father has raised me well. He loves me so much that only a man who can love me in a way that He has made me accustomed to, will do. He protects me well and hides me from danger. God's daughters are precious and precious things should be kept in velvet boxes. I had always had His protection around me even when I didn't know it. A protection that made me feel safe to leave my house or car unlocked. I had protection that allowed me to get up from a table and leave my phone there. In fact, Ansell, means "the protection of God".

Saying, Hurt not the earth, neither the sea, nor the trees, till we have sealed the servants of our God in their foreheads.

Revelation 7:3

BLINDED TO EVERYTHING

To quote Leonard Ravenhill, "when you see Jesus like that, you'll be blinded to everything else." Once I had this second encounter with Jesus, everything changed. My heart softened even further and I began to look at everyone the way that He had looked at me that night. One morning, whilst reading through the gospel of John, I found myself reading about Jesus. I was so shocked that I almost dropped the book. My Heavenly Father spent that entire morning highlighting the scriptures that talked about the blood of Christ washing away our sins and His children being marked. The words in front of me backed up my experience, as until then I didn't even know that our Lord Jesus washed the feet of His disciples.

Jesus, knowing that the Father had given all things into His hands, and that He had come from God and was going to God, rose from supper and laid aside His garments, took a towel and girded Himself. After that, He poured water into a basin and began to wash the disciples' feet, and to wipe them with the towel with which He was girded. Then He came to Simon Peter. And Peter said to Him, "Lord, are You washing my feet?"

Jesus answered and said to him, "What I am doing you do not understand now, but you will know after this."

Peter said to Him, "You shall never wash my feet!"

Jesus answered him, "If I do not wash you, you have no part with Me."

John 13:3-8

I told a few people about that second encounter but mainly kept it to myself. It was so precious that I didn't want anyone's opinions on it, let alone their pessimism. I knew some wouldn't believe me, but that didn't bother me. What bothered me was what they may say about Him. I wanted to protect His name as He protected mine, and so I kept the story to myself until one night, I had a dream. I was standing on a mountain top, overlooking a vast and grey looking world. It seemed bleak from all the way up there. Next to me was Him, in all His glory.

He looked over at me with sad eyes. "Why have you forsaken me?" He said.

My heart broke. All I wanted to do was please Him and serve Him for He had saved me from torment but what did He want me to do?

"Tell everyone," He said.

Jesus commands us to tell others of His great salvation. He wants everyone to know about Him. He suffered a horrible death so that all of mankind could be reconciled to the Father.

John 4:28

Being Raised by God

THE CALLING

My prayers morning, noon and night, are to teach me about the kingdom. I seek after the Lord daily because I am thirsty for knowledge and wisdom. Everything in my life is now from Him and I take nothing from the world itself. The home that's around me is a gift from Him, therefore I take care of it and honour it. The money in my bank account is His, therefore I spend it the way He tells me. I wouldn't dare receive something from Him and then trample it through mud. I believe that you can see how close one is to the Lord based on how they handle their possessions. When it comes from the world, it gets trampled upon even by its owner and their new garments get thrown onto the floor, their new car gets filled with empty food containers, in fact anything new that enters their house awaits its dust covered blanket. Their money is squandered on things that make them feel good for a moment and they believe that a world of debt and loans is normal.

Once saved, we are called. We cannot have one without the other. The calling cannot come before salvation and salvation cannot exist without a calling. Once saved, our

Heavenly Father speaks life over us and, just as He did at the beginning of creation, He does so with us. "Let there be light." He commands into our bodies and the Holy Spirit enters, moving through every crevice of our being, leaving no place empty. As the Holy Spirit moves within us, it begins to push out all that is not holy. It's not a comfortable process but, as the light of Christ moves through us, the darkness dispels for light cannot dwell with dark. Like the fall of Lucifer, the heavens force the evil that dwells within us out, for it cannot stay. It's impossible.

> **Then God said, "Let there be light"; and there was light. And God saw the light, that it was good; and God divided the light from the darkness. God called the light Day, and the darkness He called Night. So the evening and the morning were the first day.**
> ***Genesis 1:3-4***

Everyone is called and everyone has something unique that God has in store for them. All those who are saved, know. Whether they act on this or not is their free will, but knowing that you're called without acting upon it will torment you.

When I sit with clients and point out where God is calling them, it's always met with an extremely emotional moment. This purpose makes complete sense when you go back and look at your life before salvation, because the Lord has set you up for this very moment. If I looked over my own shoulder, I could see the burning pathway. I could see a lifelong desire to help others and I could see how it plagued me when I had no one to serve. Just like most things in life then, I always tried to do it all myself and I rushed ahead. I went after my calling before I had salvation (as so many do) and this led me down so many wrong avenues. Tarot reader, healer, medium, psychic, witch. You name it, I tried it on, but I knew I was here for something and it's why so many of those in this industry refuse to listen to me. They know they have a calling because Satan has taken that one truth, but he's wrapped it in lies, leaving those in the healing industry stuck in a web of lies, left for dead.

A year after my salvation, my Heavenly Father called me and the message hit me like lightning. So many people think that when He tells you something, He's requesting. This isn't my belief. My belief is that He is speaking life into you, just as He spoke the Earth into existence.

"Go back to the places you were and bring my children home," He said. He wasn't asking me or demanding of me, He was speaking it over me and when He speaks over us, we become it; and that day, I became it. I wanted a microphone in my hands more than anyone I knew. Making small videos online and talking to followers just wasn't going to hit the spot anymore. I needed to shout from a pulpit and cry from a stage. Anything to wake people up from their sleepy misery. I didn't know it then, but the next six months of my life would be preparation for a ministry that He made and used me for, because I could see so much darkness, even in the churches. Where was people's fire for Christ? Why weren't people talking about Satan? Why don't the children know? For Satan reaches out to steal you even from your mother's womb.

The Lord had allowed me to spend eight years in a demonic industry. I had worked with demons and entities.

I knew all their little tricks, and now the Lord was sending me back into the firing line to stand at the front, prepared to take a bullet in the name of Christ. But to be able to do this, the Lord had to begin to change me. Just like most, I didn't see I had much value in the world. I didn't know that I was able to do much to help even though I wanted to. These were all lies from the enemy that I had taken on as part of my identity. The Lord set to work on delivering me from all my entanglements and He began by showing me my value.

Although my Heavenly Father got me out of my old life, He had to also get my old life out of me. How can one possibly step into the kingdom of Heaven on Earth without first learning the lies that have been infiltrated into our precious minds? The more I learnt about such lies, the more I realised why life never quite made sense to me. This dense, heavy veil that Satan puts over us is one of deception with its only purpose to kill and destroy. But of course, like so many others, I didn't even believe in Satan. This seems so conniving when I look back, as I had so many conversations with friends and family about the evil of the world. We all discussed how demonic certain parts of the world were, and how certain industries were, yet none of us believed in Satan. We believe in Satanism but not Satan. Oh, how the veil was covering our eyes! But now it is clear that the system of this world is merely a creation from him. It traps its victims and keeps them in a life of consistently trying to catch up or chase what they think is the answer.

Satan leads you down paths that you are not yet ordained to walk, so you'll never get too far. It'll simply crumble in front of you because it was never yours, only a mirage created by him. He will trick you into selling yourself before a purchase.

He invites you into long term relationships without the commitment of marriage. He leads you into buying a home before you know how to keep it clean. He is the price of lies.

You are of your father the devil, and you choose to do your father's desires. He was a murderer from the beginning, and does not stand in the truth, because there is no truth in him. When he lies, he speaks out of his own character, for he is a liar and the father of lies.

John 8:44

When I was in the New Age industry, there was a time that I made (what felt like at the time) a lot of money. However, I was young. I didn't know how to invest it, save it, or more importantly multiply it, as our Heavenly Father does. Instead, I squandered it. I spent it on things that felt good in the moment and I spent over my means. I didn't save accordingly and I didn't use it for God's will. By the time I got back on my feet financially, after my salvation, the Lord had shown me how the kingdom of God works. He showed me how to receive from Him and multiply it. This meant that, by the time I was ready to receive a financial blessing by Heaven, I was ready to do His will with it.

It took eighteen months of deliverances for Him to release me of old habits and demonic strongholds. During that time, He taught me how to buy and sell stock, how to tithe and give well and how to receive graciously. He taught me the true value of what I was offering to those who worked with me and priced my work accordingly. He also taught me how to cook, clean and take care of myself. This all seems rather peculiar when I write it like that, but this was all done in His name. I didn't take cooking classes, but instead He taught me to slow down and enjoy the deliciousness of seeing food come to life through cooking a meal. He made me fall in love with service and serving those around me, to the point that I didn't want a home for myself, I wanted a home to serve. It became a great desire of mine to have a home where people would find rest or a spare room if there was no room at the inn. If they were growing tired or weary, my home was a shelter where they'd be greeted with freshly baked snacks or a warm meal, straight from the oven. My Heavenly Father also taught me how to clean, something with which I had always struggled.

I've lived in around thirty different houses in my life and I didn't know how to maintain, clean or take care of each house. I would make food, but not wash the dishes. I would sleep for long hours, but never make the bed. I would brush my teeth, but never wash the sink. I was living in survival mode and no matter what house I had it wouldn't stay clean. My cars were the same. No matter what car I had it wouldn't stay clean. This was how I began to spot Satan at work in my life because he won't prepare you for the blessings he offers. You'll be on a constant cycle of accumulating new things just to see them end up on the junk pile like everything else.

They will eventually end up looking like Satan's kingdom instead of God's kingdom. God's kingdom is filled with riches, jewels and pearls, everything's beautiful. It shines bright because the Lord's presence illuminates the Heavens. Satan's kingdom doesn't look like this. Satan's kingdom has filth, dust and dirt. It's covered in grime in which its gremlins can hide. Every house I ever had ended up looking like Satan's kingdom because I hadn't been taught how to take care of what I had. I could rest assured, however, that whatever God had for me He'd prepare me for it first. If he's going to bring you a home, he will first make sure you know how to clean it, how to take care of it and how to honour it. This takes patience because it's not a quick process to learn such things, but if you skip ahead with Him you'll be tempted to accept what Satan has to offer, for His blessings come fast but then end just as fast and they arrived. If you receive a blessing from Heaven, nothing can take it away. Nothing can destroy it. It's forever. If you receive a blessing from Satan, it soon gathers rot just like everything else in his kingdom.

FOLLOW THE YELLOW BRICK ROAD

I hate poverty as much as I hate Satan because poverty means that I cannot serve the kingdom. I can pray over your illness but I cannot take the bills off of your shoulders. I can listen to your concerns regarding late payments and missed bills but I cannot pay them for you. I can call you on the phone to offer you words of comfort but I cannot get on a plane to bring you the hug of the Lord. Poverty is loud, it's filthy and it's a demonic breeding ground. You cannot afford high quality foods and instead live off of cheap, processed bites posing as food but instead look like shiny, plastic objects. If you get a toothache, you must live with the pain because the dentist bill is too much to bear, and if you want to work with me, you cannot.

This was when the Lord began to expose poverty to me. I was attacked from all angles by the poor and thought they were righteous for they cannot see that, if they had more than enough to live peacefully as Jesus did, they could truly do the Lord's work. Instead, they believe that Jesus was poor because this lie will keep them bound, along with their debt and their loans. When the Lord began to raise me up financially, the first commandment I received was to pay off all my debt. At first, I didn't know how I'd do that with my measly little twenty-one pence in my bank account. I had given up everything that wasn't from Him and this had left me with nothing. I was staying with a friend who had kindly let me use one of her bedrooms and I was obeying the Lord and starting to speak out about the illusions of the New Age and how much we've been lied to. I had no car so I walked everywhere and my wardrobe would be rotated between three outfits, for that was all I had.

However, I did have the Lord and I did have His commands. I obeyed daily and always did as I was told. When I booked my first new client, I was excited to have a little money to keep me going, but the Lord had other plans. He told me to pay a debt that was hovering over me with my name on it. I did so. I then booked another client and the Lord asked me to do the same thing. Within a month, I had no debt. I had paid back all debt owed and paid back my father who had lent me some money a year prior. All I was left with was a tax bill of eighteen thousand pounds. As an average woman in the world, staying at a friend's house and unable to even buy a few outfits, I had no hope that this would pay off anytime soon, but I did know that my Heavenly Father could do it in a heartbeat. He did. Watching this was a miracle and calling the tax office to make such a payment was His work and His alone.

I was being shown a new way of living financially during this season. I would consider it the season where my Heavenly Father taught me how to be a good steward of money, which is important for all His children, for if we know not how to steward His money, we cannot obtain in. Instead, it'll go to the wicked who will squander it, steal it and use it against God's children.

One of the biggest lies that Satan has put on Christians is one of poverty and many think that if they choose Christ, they choose such poverty. People thought this of me when they heard me across multiple podcasts proclaim that I had given up all my money to follow Christ. They assumed that I had taken a vow of poverty when, really, I had made a vow to my Heavenly Father that I wouldn't take anything that wasn't from Him, and the money I was making wasn't from Him, nor were the services that I offered. My followers weren't organically from Him either so I deleted my social media platforms with over half a million followers. I gave up my home as I couldn't afford it, and sought out the kindness of friends for a place to stay. The Lord took care of me this whole time, though people looked upon me as if I was seeking a life of poverty. But I wasn't, I just wanted nothing from the world that wasn't from Him.

The more I searched for Christ in my heart, the more I naturally wanted to be like Him as we all do. As so many believed that Jesus was poor, they seek a life of poverty and find themselves bound to Satan, the prince of poverty. Without our inheritance from the Lord, we can't walk in our anointing, and what I quickly discovered was that a lot of religion taught poverty but the Lord taught wealth, and Jesus

Himself was presented with enough money to fund a ministry the moment He was born.

And when they had come into the house, they saw the young Child with Mary His mother, and fell down and worshiped Him. And when they had opened their treasures, they presented gifts to Him: gold, frankincense, and myrrh.

Luke 2:11

Before I was saved, I believed the lie of poverty as so many do. I believed that to follow Christ was to be poor and, since I had given up the money I had made in the New Age, it certainly felt like that. I also noticed the expectations of fellow followers around me. They expected me to stay within the realms of poverty and demonised anything I charged for as a service of my work. As a teacher, how dare I get paid if I love Jesus, they said. They expected me to have just enough to get by. But having just enough meant that I couldn't pay the bills of struggling friends. It meant that if a family member got sick, I couldn't assure the best care for them. It meant that I'd have nothing to leave for those who followed after me.

A good man leaves an inheritance to his children's children, but the sinner's wealth is laid up for the righteous.

Proverbs 13:22

If poverty was good, then why are we always trying to get out of it? Why does it come with worries and concerns along with a lack of sleep? So many accuse the rich of idolising money, but the poor do also. If you don't have it, it controls you. When I had little, I was constantly looking at my bank balance as my bank balance determined what I could or couldn't do. It was bondage. However, if we receive the blessings of the Lord, we are free to do what we need to do and go to the places He's calling us to go to. As far as I could see, money controlled the poor, not the rich.

> **Give to everyone what you owe them: taxes to whom taxes are due, revenue to whom revenue is due, respect to whom respect is due, honour to whom honour is due.**
>
> ***Romans 13:7***

As I began to learn more about the kingdom of God, I began to see why the Wizard of Oz was a movie constantly on repeat when I was a child. A movie in which the moral of the story was that a young woman had the ability to go home within her all along. God, being home. A movie of jewelled shoes, just as He would dress us, and a woman who follows a yellow brick road, mimicking the golden streets of heaven.

My Heavenly Father wanted me to learn to build with Him. This meant that I was to learn to build something that would stand, for I had authority over the land in which He'd given me. When He showed me my future, it was in a way that I could clearly see it was already written. It was done. He had created it and He was handing the keys over to me. I had dominion over it and, with great care, I nurtured it as Adam once did in the Garden of Eden.

> **The Lord God took the man and put him in the Garden of Eden to work it and take care of it. And the Lord God commanded the man, "You**

are free to eat from any tree in the garden but you must not eat from the tree of the knowledge of good and evil, for when you eat from it you will certainly die."

Genesis 2:15-17

When I look around now, I can see a world filled with big, empty houses. They may hold stuff but they don't hold the Holy Spirit. Things made of man but not of God. If God ever called for me to build a house, I'd not go to a supplier for bricks, shiny doors, laminated floors and square glass panels for the windows. I'd go to Bali to seek out the oldest double door as an entry point to my kitchen. I'd fly to Paris and search for the scent of old wooden floorboards to line my lounge. I'd find myself in antique auctions to exchange my resources for stained glass windows that had once given church guests quite the visionary – for now I could have that same visionary as I sipped my morning coffee.

There are so many dwellings that look shiny on the outside, but when you open the door the cheap hinge makes a noise. When you look closer, you see gaps in the floorboard due to lack of care. When you open a kitchen drawer to gain access to your appliances, the handle slips under your hand. This reminds me so much of the devil and how he operates. Offering something shiny yet nothing of value. When we build with God, it stands the test of time. Homes, churches and marriages still stand because He was there in the making. When Satan builds a house, it crumbles. It may look grand from the outside yet it mimics that of emptiness and has little character.

Unless the LORD builds the house, the builders labour in vain. Unless the LORD watches over the city, the guards stand watch in vain.

Psalms 127

So, as I began to get more comfortable in my authority, I sought after wisdom more and more. I prayed on my knees, asking to be filled with the wisdom of the Holy Spirit and the knowledge of God's kingdom. I wanted to know it all. I wanted to know how to build with Him and what that looked like. I never wanted to run ahead of Him because, like a child running out of the sight of her parents sight, it would make me unsafe. I'd spent the good part of thirty-five years running ahead, but now that I knew Him, I'd become sensitive to Him calling me back if I ran in front.

Partly, of course, I can't help it. For my Heavenly Father made me this way. He made me take leadership of my life and designed me so that I never followed a crowd for such a crowd was of Satan. He needed me this way in order for me to be able to stand on a stage and proclaim to thousands of people just how much I loved Him. My words always feel like a sonnet as I think of Him. My hands find their own gestures and usually find their way to my heart as I tell all who will listen, just how much I adore Him, and when I pray to Him it is that of a child speaking to her father and seeing Him in all His glory.

I have lost count of the number of times I have heard my mother say, "I can give you advice but I know you won't listen," and she'd be right. I wouldn't. If you knew me, you'd know that I rarely listen to anyone's advice. This was never to be rude. No, my mother raised me better than that. But worldly advice from worldly people has always felt so tainted.

The famous movie director Baz Luhrmann once said that, "advice is a form of nostalgia: dispensing it is a way of fishing the past from the disposal, wiping it off, painting over the ugly parts, and recycling it for more than it's worth."

I will always remember this. A person's advice is based on their own past and their own pain and they will tell you what to do based on what they did.

When I first told my testimony, it was on a podcast called, *God's Voice Today*. My inbox became filled with people writing in to give me their opinion of me, and this opinion was of course not one I was seeking. They seemed to have a lot of opinions too, especially around the subject of money. They were devoted Christians, yet followed Satanic teachings of poverty.

"You can't charge that! Don't you know what's happening with the economy?" one of them proclaimed.

"No," I replied. "I'm not worried about any economy because my kingdom is not of this world. I don't serve it nor do I seek its frame."

Jesus said, "My kingdom is not of this world. If it were, my servants would fight to prevent my arrest by the Jewish leaders. But now my kingdom is from another place."
John 18:36

Any individual who's worried about what the world looks like does not know such a kingdom as God's, because the Bible clearly states that God is never changing (Malachi 3:6 and Hebrews 13:8). He is the same today, tomorrow and forever; yet our economy is constantly fluctuating. This is confusing people, not to mention scaring them. That is not the work of my Heavenly Father. When I encountered Jesus, He was gold, therefore it was clear from where He came. He came from a kingdom paved with golden streets.

The great street of the city was of pure gold, like transparent glass.
Revelation 21:21

The kingdom in which I was now living was surely filled with treasures. I saw the gold in people's eyes and the treasures in a handshake. I saw beauty in the movement of the crowd. I saw God in everything. The more I saw this, the more comfortable I began to feel in high places. There's never a hurry because the Lord will shepherd you throughout the day. My Heavenly Father gives me the princess treatment. I can trust that, wherever He sends me, there will be flowers on the table, smiles in the crowd and a sense of peace in the room. God's Kingdom is royal. It's wealthy. It's luxurious. Food tastes better. Tea seems sweeter. Smiles are brighter. There's a sense of rest wherever you go.

No matter what's happening on the surface, you'll be able to feel the reassurance of your Heavenly Father. A person in stress, worry or fear, even in the name of the Lord, has taken themselves out from under His covering. Stress is from the enemy. Poverty is from the enemy. Disease is from the enemy.

The Valley of Decisions

REPRESENTING THE KINGDOM

I do believe that I've become what people may call, 'a Jesus freak'. I can't hold a conversation without Him and I certainly wouldn't dare receive a compliment because I know full well that the kind words have nothing to do with something that I've done. It's Him who's changed everything and it's Him whose eyes I see through. The more I let Jesus into my heart, the more painful this world becomes. It hurts to be in the presence of blasphemous language and it is even became painful to be around someone who spews their distaste about others. This is likely because I see that God gets edged out with every curse word and every bit of distaste.

One day, in the presence of a blasphemous woman, I noticed that it felt like tiny knives in my heart. I realised that it had been a long time since such language left my lips. I began to notice that not only was it ungodly, it was also in bad taste. If someone cannot express themselves without using a curse word in every sentence, then it appears that their intellectual development is cursed. Some people would say it's a bad habit, but I believe it is the presence of something much darker. I can sense the demonic presence with every curse word or any word that drips with disdain.

Many stay away from Christians and this is partly why. How can a Godly individual hate on another and expect those watching to be inspired to Christ? I certainly couldn't comprehend how a Christian or a follower of Christ could see someone in such a dark light. How can they find hatred in their heart? Didn't they know? Didn't they know that we wrestle not with flesh and blood but against principalities? Didn't they know that, instead of hating someone, they need to pray for them? Instead of chastising them, they need to deliver them?

For we wrestle not against flesh and blood, but against principalities, against powers, against the rulers of the darkness of this world, against spiritual wickedness in high places.

Ephesians 6:12

This was one of the first changes I noticed in myself after I had my encounters with Jesus. I didn't try to watch my language or be cautious about how I viewed people; in fact, I gave it no thought at all. I just didn't have it in me to hold grudges or to hate someone, no matter what they did to me. My Heavenly Father had shown me mercy, therefore any old trait of hate speech was plucked out of me and He showed me that we must be cautious about what we speak over our lives. How many times in the day do we proclaim an illness or a tiredness? And how many times a day do we hear people cursing their very own life? Curses such as, "this is killing me" are spoken over our lives on a daily basis and all who proclaim it, experience it. They get sicker and sicker.

I had to go through a process myself about how to use my words. My Heavenly Father slowly showed me how to use my voice with intention and not by default, causing me to say less. You see, we can chatter away and not realise the words we use. We communicate with our voice but we also declare, and we don't just declare for ourselves, we declare over others.

When we take time out of our day to use our voice to put another down, we curse them too. The hate in you may say, 'good!' But, you reap what you sow. You cannot curse the life of another without receiving the curse yourself. This means that every time you put someone down or complain about them, you're sending yourself further away from Christ, for He does not see that person as you see them. They're a precious child of God who He still wants returned to Him, whether you do or not.

When we complain about our own life and the things that seem to not be lining up the way we want them to, we fail to understand that life shouldn't align with what you want but instead what He wants. But this is where the Holy Spirit comes in. If we find ourselves desperately trying to not speak badly or to not use blasphemous language, we don't have the Holy Spirit or the Holy Spirit declaring what is. There should be no effort on your behalf. When we are filled with the Holy Spirit, these things are pushed out of us for the Holy Spirit to have a home. Many who struggle with sin have not had the baptism of the Holy Spirit yet, and this isn't found in church or a hymn, it's found in surrendering your life and your will to God.

As my words began to change, however, I began to speak more easily to others with love, no matter how they wanted to speak to me. Sometimes I'd just say nothing, for the Lord held my tongue so I couldn't curse another's life, and I felt the Holy Spirit take control of what I speak. Therefore if you wish to curse me, speak ill of me or cause harm to me, you have the free will to do so, but you won't receive it back from me.

> **You have heard that it was said, 'An eye for an eye and a tooth for a tooth.' But I tell you not to resist an evil person. But whoever slaps you on your right cheek, turn the other to him also. If anyone wants to sue you and take away your tunic, let him have your cloak also.**
>
> *Matthew 5:38-40*

"I want you to make a vow to me today," the Holy Spirit told me on one of my morning walks.

"Anything," I said in my mind, swooning.

"I need you to never apologise for saying that which I have asked you to say."

My mind was immediately filled with examples of a cancelling culture. This culture, a way of Satan making people of this world live in fear the way a narcissist roams their home, made people say things like:

- Don't take this the wrong way, but…
- I know that people will twist my words, but…
- I don't mean this, I mean that…

A world of apologies is in our midst and it comes from people who wish to please the world and the people of it, rather than please God. The Holy Spirit convicted me right there, and made sure that when I wrote books, made videos and spoke to clients, I didn't mince my words. I said what I meant and I meant what I said. I wasn't here to baby anyone, but instead to be so bold and direct that it triggered people into an awakening, for the walking dead amongst us perk up only when offended.

The most luxurious God is the God I know. He raised me well and taught me greatly in fact, one of the many precious paths He led me down was right after I was saved. He began to show me, as a loving parent would, how to dress myself, how to walk, how to talk and how to rest as He does. I noticed that, just as my father taught me how to walk and talk, so did He; but this time it was ever so different. I now represent His kingdom and this role I take very seriously. The way I speak, act and dress, tells everyone about the God I serve, and if I buy my food from low priced places then people will think that the God I serve lacks generosity. If I throw on an unkept outfit or spend most of my days in sweatpants then people will think I serve a depressive God. If I walk around without a smile on my face as a sign of basking in His glory, then people will think I serve a God who lacks presence.

This is why one of the first things he convicted me of was what I wore. He never scolded me and never shamed me. That's the enemy's job. What He did was to hold me so tightly that I began to feel like I was actually special. You see, we miss this so much in the world. We get thrown out in the cold whether we like it or not, and we learn to fend for ourselves. It doesn't matter how loving your family was, at some point you'll have to face the cold harsh seasons that this world offers. You'll be lied to, cheated on and stolen from, and the longer we encounter this, not only do we see it as normal but we also begin to think we deserve it.

My Heavenly Father removed this from me quite promptly and, the more I felt His love, the more I naturally moved away from clothing that was too revealing or too tight. When you begin to see yourself as He sees you, you begin to feel protective over what He gave you. This body is special and what is special should be protected. Therefore, what I began to feel more comfortable in were soft fabrics and a modest taste. He delivered me from the worldly view of a woman's body, which is mainly to be provocative.

Although I was never one to show off my body, I did once believe that the more desirable I was, the more wanted I'd be. I thought that being lusted upon made me worthy. But as I see this now, to be lusted upon is to be invaded and this is something I simply won't participate in.

There was a movement that I was once a part of in the New Age, which teaches women to be liberated in their flesh. It encourages them to love their bodies and to not be afraid to show them off. In some of the local circles (when I lived in Australia) it was common to hear of Women's Circles where they gathered around under the moon and danced naked like it was some sort of ritual. But I felt so terrible that I just didn't feel comfortable taking part. At the time, as I was surrounded by so many 'liberated' women, I couldn't help but think that there was something wrong with me for not wanting to take part. In fact, I thought that I had some kind of inner work to do to be more confident in my body. The truth was that I was actually very confident in my body but I certainly didn't feel comfortable showing it off to the world. God was protecting me.

To put your body out to the world to be lusted upon will create so many strongholds that most women don't know what to do with it. They can't understand the sadness and the emptiness, when what is really happening under the surface is that they've been tricked. The enemy uses them like puppets on a string and displays them in a window in public because he doesn't want them ever to know how special they really are.

Honestly? The world is riddled with empty, naked women screaming liberal things, but then they return home to sob on an empty couch.

For everything in the world – the lust of the flesh, the lust of the eyes, and the pride of life – comes not from the Father but from the world.
1 John 2:16

PAYING THE PRICE

I could write a sonnet about fabric. The smell of leather as you walk through the streets of Florence, the feel of chiffon fabrics in Paris or the gold buttons anointing the streets of Piccadilly Market. I've never been one to enjoy fast fashion. I even resent the idea of putting cheap fabric against my skin, causing it to create an itch that only the devil wants to scratch. I see the loose threads of cheap garments hanging from its owner's sleeve with little purpose and its buttons falling like Babylon.

I've never enjoyed cheap coffee and I've never seen the value in a bargain, because something in me could recognise value over price. There's no such thing as a bargain. Buy cheap food and you'll reap disease. Buy cheap clothes and you'll reap a skin rash. Buy cheap shoes and you'll reap a blister. But even something of expense can lose value. As soon as a label is placed on the outside of the garment, it immediately loses value for something of such value that needs to label itself, is immediately throwing itself onto the pile of lesser value, because value is silent. Just the way a woman wears tight clothes or reveals her breasts, stomach or thighs through her garments, there is no value where there is no mysticism.

I can also see the value in something old instead of something new, as the enemy ever continues to move through the world. Fast fashion, fast food, a fast life. Yet God is not this. I am willing to pay triple the price to have something of quality, because I'm not willing to pay the hidden price.

When we don't know Him, and when we are in the claw of the enemy, we cannot seek value in fact, we can't even see it. We cannot see the hidden price, only the surface price.

"What a bargain!" you'll say.

"But what is the hidden cost?" I'll ask.

I despise going into my wardrobe and not being able to write a poem for each garment that hangs there. I want to be able to run my fingers down the seams and feel the admiration that I have for that garment. I choose pieces wisely. I choose pieces specifically for me. There's a story behind all that I own. I choose my organic coffee wisely. I choose my restaurants wisely. And so God once asked me, why do I not treat myself this same way? Why do I not see myself with the same value that I seek in the world?

> **But you trusted in your beauty and used your fame to become a prostitute. You lavished your favours on anyone who passed by and your beauty became his. You took some of your garments to make gaudy high places, where you carried on your prostitution. You went to him, and he possessed your beauty. You also took the fine jewellery I gave you, the jewellery made of my gold and silver, and you made for yourself male idols and engaged in prostitution with them. And you took your embroidered clothes to put on them, and you offered my oil and incense before them. Also the food I provided for you – the flour, olive oil and honey I gave you to eat – you offered as fragrant incense before them. That is what happened, declares the Sovereign Lord.**
>
> ***Ezekiel 16:15-19***

I never used to see my value, though everyone around me did, and there seemed to be a pattern in my bloodline. So many saw my value, but didn't want to pay the price of it. I saw this in my friendships, romances, and even the general public who found my work. Most mornings, I would wake up with a full inbox of strangers from all around the world sending me a thesis on their life events, but not wanting to pay the price of having a phone call with me. They wanted what I had but weren't willing to pay the price. Whether it was a pound or ten thousand pounds, no exchange was made or offered. They would keep showing up, wanting more and more, as much as they could get their hands on; but never making a sacrifice themselves. Unless there's a sacrifice somewhere, you get nothing. There's no initiation that will take place without an offer, and those who attempted to take from me without this, got very little. It didn't matter if I responded and took time out of my day to help, the problem never resolved because, without the sacrifice, they could not hear me.

This is the world we live in. Everyone wants a bargain. Everyone wants something for free, but you can't get something for free. There's a price that you have to pay and I paid that price when I gave my life to Jesus. I know not what it's like to spend an evening watching television, but I do know what it's like to stay up all night with my Heavenly Father and read the Bible with Him. I know not what it's like to go to a drive-through McDonald's or to buy a chocolate bar from the corner shop of an evening; but I do know what it's like to spend a whole day preparing a meal, laying the table, lighting candles and sitting down with fine china plates to eat dinner with the Holy Spirit. I know not what it's like to have a husband hold onto me every night in comfort and safety, but I do know what it's like to be tucked in and held protected by Jesus as I sleep.

I receive so many messages from men and women who tell me that they'd love to have the experiences that I have had, and that they too want a relationship with the Lord, as I do. Some even proclaim jealousy. But they have not yet paid the price. I do not live in this world, I am just of it. I don't buy into distractions. I don't scroll on social media. I don't go to sports games. I don't gossip or speak words of unkindness. I don't lie. I don't cheat and I don't steal. Every day, I am awoken by God (ever so gently) and I am called to pray and worship. Sometimes I read scripture. Sometimes I read a book all about Him. I spend the day writing about Him, talking about Him, experiencing Him. A moment doesn't go by where I don't seek Him or follow Him. I don't make choices; but instead, obey. I don't go to parties and I don't watch movies. Why would I watch people dressing up, pretending to be someone else, all in the name of entertainment? Why would I choose this when I could be with Him? Do you live the same way?

As soon as I paid the price and gave my life to God, I repented. I apologised to Him for taking something that He saw as so precious and throwing it to the swine. One of the first sentences I ever heard from my Heavenly Father was…

Do not give dogs what is sacred; do not throw your pearls to pigs. If you do, they may trample them under their feet, and turn and tear you to pieces.
Matthew 7:6

I began to hold those around me by the same standard, though messages and calls still poured in.

Laura, Laura, Laura! Help me. Save me. Love me.

These others saw the value that I carried. They saw wisdom for which I'd prayed. They saw the value I could offer. But who was willing to pay the price?

In the past, I had adapted myself to meet the needs of others. I'd adapted my worth, my time and my schedule to meet the needs of someone else, just so I could have that client, that friend or that man. Constantly bending and reshaping myself to fit into the lives of others where I didn't belong. Men had used every piece of me, just like the devil does with all of us. They had used up every single piece of me, but when the cheque came and it was time to pay with commitment, marriage or family, they left me to bleed out.

I have given my life to Jesus, the man who never left me to die. He picked me up, after so many had discarded me, and carried me home. I paid the price with my own life and that is the price those who seek me must pay too.

My price is my protection for I do not come cheap. There's a cost. And what eventually will be a metaphorical value, can become a physical one. My Heavenly Father will simply not allow my services to run cheap. This acts as a barrier of protection because most people will pay a penny to seek help, but I am not for everyone. If something of this world is accessible to everyone then it contains no value. But of course the demons in people feast on judgement and criticism. The people who stop by to watch my testimony or my teachings can have a problem with money. They know of God but don't know Him personally. Their feet are caught in the trap of the enemy's poverty and they are seeking a bargain. They want a discount, but I am not willing to do half the work for half their price. My price protects me from swine and, instead, makes me specific for those who are a witness to the value. I have been given the freedom to only work with the best quality people. It isn't just that they can afford to purchase, it is that they can't afford *not to*. The price to not work with me is more expensive than the price to work with me, because they see the hidden costs of walking away from me.

When we walk into a designer clothing store, we recognise that the price equates to the value, so why don't we see it in people? Everyone wants a quick fix and everyone wants a bargain. If you live your life looking for bargains, you'll find the devil waiting for you. You'll be surrounded by a house filled with stuff, waiting to gather dust so demons can make a home in it. You'll have hoards of clothes you'll never wear and a wardrobe filled with clothes that no longer fit, leaving trails of nostalgia where they hang. Your fridge will be filled with foods of little nutrition and cheap ingredients, leaving your body starving for more. This is all a breeding ground for the devil to feast, so do not give precious things to those who know not what you offer.

Later I passed by, and when I looked at you and saw that you were old enough for love, I spread the corner of my garment over you and covered your naked body. I gave you my solemn oath and entered into a covenant with you, declares the Sovereign Lord, and you became mine. I bathed you with water and washed the blood from you and put ointments on you. I clothed you with an embroidered dress and put sandals of fine leather on you. I dressed you in fine linen and covered you with costly garments. I adorned you with jewellery: I put bracelets on your arms and a necklace around your neck, and I put a ring on your nose, earrings on your ears and a beautiful crown on your head. So you were adorned with gold and silver; your clothes were of fine linen and costly fabric and embroidered cloth. Your food was honey, olive oil and the finest flour. You

became very beautiful and rose to be a queen. And your fame spread among the nations on account of your beauty, because the splendour I had given you made your beauty perfect, declares the Sovereign Lord.
Ezekiel 16:8-14

A CALL TO SACRIFICE

I always get so excited when God asks to spend the day with me. He knows me so well. He knows that having a day out with my father when I was little meant so much to me. We would walk around old ruined castles, eating ice cream that my mother strictly told him I wasn't allowed.

"Don't tell your Mum!" he'd say, though she always knew.

This was one of my favourite things to do with my father, so when my Heavenly Father began to invite me to spend my days of rest with Him, I could bounce off the walls with excitement.

On one such day, I immediately ran upstairs, got myself dressed, chose the bow for my hair, grabbed my things, and ran out the door. I listened to my music on my twenty-minute walk into my local town to find my favourite seat available at my favourite coffee shop. God is good.

There, I was indulging within the pages of a Rees Howells book when I reached a chapter that talked about being anointed with the Holy Spirit. I noticed that, although I had built a beautiful relationship with God and I had beautiful encounters with Jesus, I had yet to really know what it meant to have the Holy Spirit dwelling within me. I understood the concept, and I understood that I certainly had the Holy Spirit moving through me, but was it moving through all of me?

As I sat there with Him, reading the words of these pages, I felt the call – are you willing to sacrifice it all?

I didn't understand what that would look like or what it even really meant, but in that moment I said under my breath, "Yes, Heavenly Father, I'll give it to you, just show me what you need me to do."

The next few days unravelled beautifully. I got to witness incredible testimonies and incredible sermons by people explaining what it meant to give your life over fully. Some people talked about picking up the cross daily, but my Heavenly Father wasn't referring to picking up a cross daily. This was about never putting it down.

I must admit that I found the idea completely romantic because I had always lived my life in sacrifice. It was in me to sacrifice. I'd sacrifice my life so many times. I'd given up beautiful homes to live in the home of a man. I'd even given up my country to give my life to men in the past. I'd given my life, my love, my whole self over to them, only to be dropped at the very last minute. Every experience was so painful, yet I couldn't not be this way. Sacrifice was built into me. I couldn't be distant in love and I couldn't just give a small percentage of myself. I always gave my all, but no man ever paid the full price of commitment to have me, except for Jesus. Jesus wanted all of me for His kingdom, so how could a woman say 'no' to such an offer? I'm a people pleaser and I seek to please God.

The Sunday following this particular day, I found myself in my usual church service. I was standing up next to my friend with my hands in the air, singing and praising Him.

As I worshiped, the voice of the Holy Spirit entered into my heart, and He said, "Are you willing to go to the places so few have gone? If you give everything up, and give yourself to me, I will meet all your needs. I will take care of everything. I will provide for you and I will protect you. If you give yourself to me, I will be your source of everything. I don't want you to take anything from this world but, instead, take it from me."

Tears fell down my cheeks and His words moved around in my heart. My answer was 'yes'.

As I looked around the room, families were surrounding me. Married couples were holding hands, groups of friends were huddled together, though I'd always been the loner. I'd always been independent. I never sought out the advice or opinions of others. I only sought out my own and, if I'd known God when I was little, I'd have sought out His. The more I looked at myself, the more I realised that the way I was designed, the way He had made me and the life He had given me, had actually set me up for a life of complete dedication to Him and only him.

I'm not good with distractions. This is why I don't own a TV and why I don't scroll on social media. If I'm listening to that then I cannot hear Him. I like to be present with the people I love and present with my Heavenly Father for it is a privilege to know Him. In my heart, there has sometimes been a slight fear of the unknown. But when I don't really know what something looks like, or I don't know how to do it, He tends to help me. He calls us into things that we cannot do to force us to lean on Him and He qualifies those He calls rather than calling those qualified.

That night, after I returned home, I got into bed early. Something in me didn't feel great. I can only describe it as a feeling of grief or mourning. But then my heart reminded me of the times that I used to miss my father. My father would travel a lot. He would go away for months at a time and I'd miss him so much that I'd feel my heart ache. There would be a nostalgic feeling in my heart, and it was similar to the way I felt that night. Although I couldn't quite put my finger on it at the time, I now know that I was grieving Laura Ansell, the woman who was born into the flesh of this world. The girl who used to want to wear pink jelly shoes around the house and high heels outside of the house, despite being five years old. The girl who used to match her hair bow to the frill of her sock. The girl who once felt so alone and so lost. The girl who sought out traveling, who chased people for a scrap of love. The girl who thought she had to be something or be someone to be seen. She was going away that night and she couldn't come back. When we're reborn, we really are born new in Christ. But what we don't think about is that we must die in the flesh. Many talk about dying in the flesh daily, but this implies there is flesh to die upon waking. The Lord was showing me something more. He was showing me a life where there was no flesh to die, for it had already been given.

With all my pondering about sacrificing my life and what that might look like, my eyes grew weary and, that evening, I found myself slumping into bed dreadfully early with my Heavenly Father covering me.

In the early hours of the morning, when it was still dark outside, I was woken. At first, I thought someone had entered my bedroom and switched the light on, but as I came to my senses I could see the light was much brighter than the little bulb that hovered over my bed. Had someone come in with a torch to shine in my face? I began to awaken more as I felt into my body, which was all cosy under my pink velvet bedding, only to feel that I wasn't fully in it. I could feel my body vibrating, though I was hovering several centimetres above it. The only thing familiar in that moment was an everlasting, ever protruding feeling of love. It was Jesus.

I tried to turn my head to look at Him, yet the golden light was so bright I physically couldn't. I was only able to glimpse at Him for a moment before He put me back into a deep sleep.

The next morning when I rose, something was very different. There was a sense of reassurance in me now that I was truly walking with Him. The grief that I had felt over the life I had once led, and the life I had once wanted, was gone. I knew, deep down, that the earthly, flesh part of me that was born in 1989, died that night, and Jesus had come to meet me at this metaphorical death. I could now walk with reassurance that, when the rest of me were to be called home one day in the future, He would be there again, for He knows me well.

Not everyone who says to Me, 'Lord, Lord,' shall enter the kingdom of heaven, but he who does the will of My Father in heaven. Many will say to Me in that day, 'Lord, Lord, have we not prophesied

in Your name, cast out demons in Your name, and done many wonders in Your name?' And then I will declare to them, 'I never knew you; depart from Me, you who practice lawlessness!

Matthew 7:21-23

40 Days in the Wilderness

FILLED WITH THE HOLY SPIRIT

My first encounter with the Holy spirit was during a forty day fast. It began when I felt something significant wash over me. It was a coolness in my body that I had never before experienced. I recognised when God spoke to me, because when he did my body froze. I recognised when Jesus spoke to me, because I'd feel the love emanating from him. But this coolness washing over me, this sense of peace and softness, rather than feeling like gold it felt like silver. Instead of being like the sun, it felt like the moon.

At first, I didn't know what was happening, only the call to lay down. As I did, the feeling washed from my toes to my nose. I felt myself lift out of my body, and that I was like two people. My hands felt huge, like I had the hands of a man. I felt this silver light all around me and an overwhelming peace. I'm quite a fidgeter, but I didn't move a muscle for twenty minutes as I lay on my bed, all the while knowing and learning that this was my first encounter with the Holy Spirit.

At the time, Lent was fast approaching and I knew that my Heavenly Father would call me to give something up. In my worldly mind, I thought that I could give up something like coffee, as I loved it so much, but God had other plans.

He wanted me to eat only one meal a day for forty days. As I realised this, the Holy Spirit's feeling of peace washed over me, as it always does when He speaks to me too, but I was also met with a feeling of concern. I had once been invited to do a similar fast for just a few days by a friend of mine, and I didn't even make it past the first day. How was I meant to do this for forty days?

It became clear rather quickly that what God leads us into will ease, as He has sent the invitation. An invitation sent by man or created by us holds difficulty. But not when He sends it.

So I settled into the idea and obeyed. I told very few people, only those who needed to know, as I would be turning down any invitations to brunches, lunches and dinners. I'd not be partaking in midnight snacks or daily grazing. I was dedicated, as I knew that these forty days with my Heavenly Father were crucial, because forty is such a significant number. My Heavenly Father read the scriptures in my mind and highlighted the transformation that forty days would create.

- Jesus fasted for forty days in the wilderness after His baptism before facing temptations by the devil.
- After His resurrection, Jesus appeared to his disciples for forty days before ascending to heaven.
- Moses spent forty days and forty nights on Mount Sinai receiving the Ten Commandments.
- The Israelites wandered in the wilderness for forty years.
- Elijah travelled for forty days and forty nights to Mount Horeb.

Now it was my turn. It was clear that my Heavenly Father had work for me to do. I knew I was stepping into my own ministry and that this fast would prepare me in some way; although of course, I didn't know how. That was only for Him to know.

I did know that many lived this way daily; but for me, it was a real adjustment. I still had many old fears left over from my teenage years of having disordered eating patterns. I'd go so long without eating that I'd become afraid that I'd fall over.

For the first week of my fast, this fear arose and I was able to give it to Him as I should have done when I was sixteen. I began to enjoy the freedom that not eating constantly brought me. I had no distractions, only Him. I could hear Him clearer and I felt lighter in my body for my daily walks. My body was graciously preparing itself for the Holy Spirit.

THE SPIRIT OF GREED

I began to notice the workings of the Holy Spirit in my spiritual body. I noticed that the longer I fasted, the more He filled me up. The more He filled me up, the more He exposed the hidden chambers within my spirit. Anything dark that once was hidden, was no longer able to hide. Not by coincidence, my friend, who was on her fast from screen time, began to witness similar things. It would appear, although not biblical to my knowledge, that demons lose their hiding place around day twenty of a fast.

Around that twenty-day point, as I was laying in my bed, I saw the image of something that took a moment to place. What was I seeing?

In front of me, I saw a large man, except he wasn't really a man. His stature was large and distorted. He did look human, yet it appeared that he was only trying to be. As I focused more, I noticed his head. It was not the head of a man but something else. A swine.

The spirit shrieked, convulsed him violently and came out. The boy looked so much like a corpse that many said, "He's dead."

But Jesus took him by the hand and lifted him to his feet, and he stood up. After Jesus had gone indoors, his disciples asked him privately, "Why couldn't we drive it out?"

He replied, "This kind can come out only by prayer."
Mark 9:26-29

"Reveal yourself," I said to the swine, knowing that in him doing so, he could be cast out. "What are you?"

"Greed," he responded.

I went cold. I found myself gazing at him with distaste as he unravelled himself and all his works right in front of me.

The abyss of loneliness and emptiness that I had known so well in the past had been an open door to one of the seven deadly sins. Greed, being one of them, had taken hold of my emptiness then, as it seemed to be his most favourite place. A place where he was desperate, as much as I felt I was, to be filled. He cannot be filled with the Holy Spirit, only stuff. And he had filled himself through me. He had made me greedy. He had made me impatient. I had been a woman who always wanted to race ahead and had burnt myself out doing so. I rarely followed God's plan and timeline for me and fell over every time I ran ahead.

This demon had walked right in through the open door of the abyss and made himself at home in my life and I didn't even know it. He covered my ears with psoriasis (something I suffered from for many years) so that I couldn't not hear his calls, but instead I had followed them blindly thinking they were mine. I'd indulged in pleasure and chasing material things. I couldn't get enough clothes, enough shoes, enough money or enough friends to fill this empty pit. I couldn't move fast enough. This demon was like a salesman who tries to make you sign the contract immediately so you don't have time to think about what you're signing up for. Even my eating disorder in the past was greed. I want to be thin *now!* Always in a hurry, always falling over and always having to pick myself up. In fact, my life had been a merry-go-round of run, fall and get up. It was exhausting. There was always a clean-up process for my life and my family would always say, 'here she goes again'.

But after I lay there, watching a review of my whole life from this demon of Greed, I climbed out of bed and dropped to my knees.

Dear Heavenly Father,

I am so sorry. I am so sorry that I chased things of the material world when all I needed was you. I'm so sorry that I ran ahead so many times that I ran out of your sight. Lord, I know that you need to see me at all times as all loving parents do, but I have disobeyed time and time again. Lord, I am sorry. I ask you for your forgiveness today and I beg for mercy. I pray, in the name of Jesus and with His blood, that you please deliver me from this demon of Greed. Lord, I cannot live with this emptiness. Unveil me in your presence and show me my sins. Lord, take this from me for it is too heavy to carry. Deliver me from the spirit of Greed and close the door. I repent. I apologise. Lord, forgive me, please. Please close this door in the mighty name of Jesus.

Amen.

Greed is deadly. It's named as one of the cardinal sins because of the destruction that they create in one's life, along with the simple fact that it will distract you from the assignment you have. They lead to diseases, loneliness, disconnection, depression, tiredness and any other thing that can be so deathly destroying that you don't have a second in the day to seek God or to understand why you're here and what He wants you to do, leading you to more loneliness. An individual who is not following the calling on their life is surely depressed. Surely lost. Surely long forgotten.

Greed, Gluttony, Lust, Wrath, Pride, Sloth and Envy. They hide in the darkest places that only the Holy Spirit can find. They intertwine themselves and confuse their hosts, keeping you wondering what seems to be happening to your life. You know that this life was not the plan for you. You feel it deep down yet you cannot put your finger on it.

In my case, I searched high and low. I searched in the tarot cards, in the spells, in the psychics and mediums. I searched my childhood. I searched my femininity. I searched from country to country, seeking the answer to my torment when it was hidden within me the whole time. No one, not a single person in my spiritual journey, ever told me to read the bible, for this book is a doctrine on how to live our life God's way. It's the blueprint of Heavenly success and fulfillment, and absolutely has nothing to do with religion as I once thought. The answer was hidden in its pages but was hidden away from me under diseased skin, over indulgence, plane trips, shoes shopping, destructive romances and all kinds of things. I sought but never found.

It was Jesus, who found me, thank the Lord and praise God.

Suppose one of you has a hundred sheep and loses one of them. Doesn't he leave the ninety-nine in the open country and go after the lost sheep until he finds it? And when he finds it, he joyfully puts it on his shoulders and goes home. Then he calls his friends and neighbours together and says, 'Rejoice with me; I have found my lost sheep.' I tell you that in the same way there will be more rejoicing in heaven over one sinner who repents than over ninety-nine righteous persons who do not need to repent.

Luke 15:3-7

THE CURSE OF CAIN

The longer I fasted, the more I felt myself dance with the Holy Spirit. His fire was ignited in me and I wished to live no different. I was high on the Holy Spirit. Blessed was I and blessed was my life. His magnificence was the glory to my life. I could write about Him all day. I could sit with Him all day. I wanted tea parties with Him so I could use my Royal Albert tea set and I wanted Him to read the bible to me. When He read it, I saw things within it that I could never see on my own. Without Him, life was so dull. He made everything seem romantic in a way, and if it weren't for Him this book wouldn't exist. I simply couldn't write something so beautifully. He moved my body, spoke over my life and adjusted me according to where He needed me. I began to look at my life so differently and I couldn't help but notice differences in the life I had with God versus the life I had had before Him. Once lonely, but now surrounded by people. Once awkward around new people, but now curious. Once addicted to late night snacks and sweet treats, but now uninterested. Once overweight, but now just right. Once tired, but now energised. My life was becoming what He wanted and my will was no longer there.

One evening during my forty-day fast, I was called to step it up. He called for me to have no meal for three days. This meant that the one little meal I was enjoying daily would now go down to zero. I felt the call from God as if He were gesturing to me from across the room.

"Come on, come on," it felt like he was saying, lovingly.

His huge, fatherly love always wins me over, sod I began to wonder what was about to happen. My Heavenly Father had indeed called me into this forty-day walk with Him and I was already seeing overwhelming changes, revelations of my ministry and deliverances from things that were deep rooted in my life. What was left?

Of course, I obeyed. Who could say 'no' to Papa?

The first twenty-four hours were easy, as I had been doing this for twenty days already. But once I reached forty-eight hours, something began to show itself. A vagabond.

And the Lord said unto Cain, Where is Abel thy brother? And he said, I know not: Am I my brother's keeper? And he said, What hast thou done? The voice of thy brother's blood crieth unto me from the ground. And now art thou cursed from the earth, which hath opened her mouth to receive thy brother's blood from thy hand; When thou tillest the ground, it shall not henceforth yield unto thee her strength; a fugitive and a vagabond shalt thou be in the earth.

Genesis 4:9-12

A vagabond spirit is a curse and it can run in the family for generations, tormenting all it seeks. This spirit, also known as the orphan spirit, is a wandering spirit, causing all those it lusts after to live a life of circles. Same story, same pattern, but a different day. It causes its victims to go from relationship to relationship, job to job, or church to church. It creates restlessness in oneself and seeks to tire you out. Whenever you get close to something, it's ripped away. If you're close to getting married, the wedding will fall through. If you're getting close to a financial goal, something will collapse. If you're close to getting a promotion, someone else will swoop in and claim it. No matter how close you get, it's taken. This is the vagabond spirit. It's clingy, needy and can only be removed by its own death. God's intention, now that I could see it, was to starve it to death in me though a fast.

That night, I said my evening prayers and shimmied under my covers. As I began to get comfortable, the presence of someone entered the room. The moment I saw her, I knew exactly who she was, but I had not thought about her since I was a teenager. She was the young girl who I had woken up to one evening when I was fifteen years old. The blonde girl with long pigtails and buckled shoes was back in the room. She crouched down by my bed and stared into me, not at me. I began to have flashbacks of this creature and remembered her story. Thinking she was a ghost, I had once sensed the story of this little orphan girl. Her parents had passed on and she was left all alone. No one to run to, no one to call. This story was wrapped around her.

Now I wondered what this demon really looked like. I knew she was not a young girl but simply posing as one, likely trying to befriend me when I was little by posing as someone my age. It had worked thus far, but now that season was over. This was the orphan spirit that had been tormenting me for most of my life, causing me to run in circles, lose things and people in whenever I began to get comfortable. She left me in a constant fight or flight, waiting for the next thing to collapse and fall through.

The vagabond spirit, as I then learnt in my prayer time with my Heavenly Father that night, is a demon that prays on the lonely. Children who move around a lot (as I did) and therefore don't connect with people for long periods of time, become lonely. When we move from school to school or house to house, we stop seeking connection because we know that it won't last anyway. I knew this feeling all too well and, as I got older and sought out a lifestyle of travel, I rarely made time for people because I knew I'd be moving within a year and I hated goodbyes. This made me an isolated woman and caused onlookers of my life to see me as flighty and I cannot blame them.

However, my life now was different. I noticed that, as I had given my life to God, I was no longer lonely, I was surrounded by people.

"I have a life now!" I said to my friend one evening as I wrapped up my week of church, bible study sessions and dinner with friends. This was a whole new world for me. It had been so long since I had stayed in one place, but now this insatiable desire to stay put in my favourite little village in the Cotswolds was in me. I wasn't going anywhere. I had no desire to travel, move around or anything of the sort. It could only be God's work.

He also began to weave commitments in my life – something the Vagabond spirit blocks. Due to the curse of flightiness, I rarely committed to anything and it had been years since I had. As I was self-employed, I could follow my own schedule; but now I was going to church every Sunday and did volunteer work every Tuesday. My life was following a schedule designed by Him. I even noticed that when I caught a cold one week, I still showed up for all I said I would. I did podcast interviews in between sneezes, and spoke to clients with my handkerchief in hand. Nothing was stopping me from doing what I said I was going to do. Having myself filled with the Holy Spirit was pushing out the curse and, by the time that I got half way through my forty-day fast, they were all being exposed. I could see the importance of Jesus asking for the name of Legion (Mark 5:9). We need to identify what is there to remove it and the moment I saw that girl and she was no longer hidden in my blood, bones and skin, was the moment I knew it was over. It was the final push. God had moved me so gently with His hands into a life of commitment, stability and growth; and now the curse working against me most of my life was exposed. Hallelujah and good riddance, I say.

As I lay in my bed being watched by this spirit, I began to pray.

Dear Heavenly Father,

I call on you to break the chains and curses on and around my life in the mighty name of Jesus. May His blood cast a wide net around my life, past, present and future and may its power dispel and collapse all strongholds that remain in my life. Lord, I break contracts of any Vagabond spirits that are in my midst, including the ones I cannot see, and I break these in the mighty name of Jesus. Any curses that have reached my friends or family members, I ask you to expose them now in the mighty name of Jesus. I ask you to adjure me like Jesus as you showed us in Acts 19:13. Lord, you are the only one. No one can do this but you and so I ask you now, Heavenly Father, to save me once again. You're the only one, Lord, you're the only one.

I pray this in the mighty name of Jesus.

Amen

I sang the Lord's praises until I felt the girl fade from the room. She got smaller and smaller the more I proclaimed my life for the Lord. The bigger I felt Him in my heart, the smaller she got. I was so excited to see the Lord paint a new life for me. So much juiciness was waiting around the corner for me and the curiosity of what life could become now that this wasn't waiting for me. I have never been someone to shy away from hard work and, now that I worked for the Lord, I felt even more fire. What would my life become if I could finally reap what I had sowed all these years?

Delivered

MATCH MADE IN HELL

There was a time in my career where I believed in the Twin Flame theory. When you research this, it will tell you that: "the "twin flame" theory, rooted in new-age spiritualism, suggests a profound, intense soul connection where two people are believed to be halves of the same soul, often described as a "mirror soul" or "other half".

This is a concept that's known worldwide and, although I don't recommend you research it as it comes with so many strongholds, it's important to shine the light of Christ upon it. For four years, I believed that there was a person in the world who was my twin flame, and I would feel a magnetic pull towards him. This pull was not wrapped in peace but in pain. I used to read tarot cards trying to understand what he was up to or what he was doing and how he felt about me, because he certainly wasn't telling me. It was four years of up and down chaos. It was four years of longing for someone or for something. It was four years of disappointment. It was four years of heartbreak. It was four years of strongholds and, in that time, I would fantasise about him. I would visualise him. I would see us together, thinking that this was helping us to find a path in order for us to be together.

As the years went on, and as I broke free of those strongholds, I remember looking back and seeing that all of my relationships since that particular relationship seemed cursed. I had not had a single successful relationship since that time and, whenever I was close to finding a relationship, it would break down at the last minute right in front of my eyes. Once upon a time I'd had beautiful relationships, then everything seemed cursed.

On day thirty of my fast, I saw something unexpected. I thought that because I had been delivered from so many oppressions and strongholds, I was done. But I was wrong. Demons always seem to show themselves to me at night, even for clients. I will see them appear right in front of me or dream about them, because God has given me the ability to see in the dark. And that particular night, as I was laying there, I feel the presence of something on my back. What looked like a gargoyle seemed to be cuddled up behind me, smiling and content. It was holding me around my shoulders, around my neck, and its legs wrapped around my waist. At first glance, I was uncomfortable with its latching, though it was feeling quite the opposite. It was so comfortable that I could see it had been there for years. And as I turned around and asked who it was, he proclaimed he was my husband. You can imagine the horror!

The next three days were a physical war between the Lord and him, with me sandwiched in between. That night I rebuked him in Jesus' name, and I felt the weight on my shoulders lift. But the next day I began to notice a cough emerge. I felt fine, yet my body couldn't stop coughing all day. I was expelling something out of my breath. I thought nothing of this because I knew about deliverance at this stage and was all too aware that demons leave through the air because Satan is referred to as the price of the air.

In which you once walked, according to the prince of the power of the air, the spirit that is now at work in the sons of disobedience.

Ephesians 2:2

The day after, I woke up in torment. I felt pain from my nose to my toes. My muscles ached, my joints ached, my teeth hurt, my hair hurt. The nerves on my body were standing on end. I spent the entire day sleeping. I couldn't eat, I couldn't drink, I couldn't move. I slept for twenty hours and, in the four that I was awake, I was in a dizzy haze, praying through.

That night, as I fell asleep, I dreamt, and although I can't tell you the full extent of the dream, I can tell you it was filled with fire-breathing dragons that fell from castles on clifftops to their death. The dream ended with me looking at a man who, although he seemed to hate me in the dream, was in fact my husband in it. He was tall with fair hair and wore a crucifix around his neck. In the dream, I walked away from him. I told him I was done and I knew I meant it. Nothing pulled me back towards him and nothing grabbed me. I simply walked away.

When I woke up the next day, I felt a million times better. It's amazing to me that someone can be so ill one day and so well the next. I knew it was a deliverance because my body needed little time to recover. I prayed to the Lord for wellness and for strength. As I drank my morning tea, my Heavenly Father began to unveil what had happened.

Years of fantasising about a situation, and about a man, had invited in a spirit husband. The New Age tells us to visualise, so of course that's what I did. I used to visualise us being married and living happily ever after. I used to make up scenarios in my head that gave me hope so I didn't have to face the truth. He just wasn't that into me!

This spirit husband began lurking around me, watching my every move. Watching me cry at night, missing this person. Watching me put my life on hold in case this man decided he wanted to be with me. I was the perfect victim for such a demon.

In the spirit world, he said to me, "it's okay, I want you." Thus this spirit husband had claimed time over my life and every relationship after that never worked because he was always standing in the way. He wanted me more than anyone. He would feed off of my energy. He would make sure that I couldn't ever be in a real relationship because this would push him aside. He had a stronghold on my life. That chapter of my life had brought in a curse on all romance and on all love.

As I reached day thirty of my fast, this demon spirit became more and more obvious. He attacked mainly at night and I'd be woken from my sleep as it tried to either strangle me or sexually assault me. Every night, I prayed for the same thing. I prayed for this spirit to be unveiled and, as the nights grew longer and the attacks grew stronger, I knew I was getting close.

One night, I fell into a deep sleep. In my dream, I lay in bed, half asleep, when a young man walked into the room. In the dream, he appeared to be my husband and he looked a lot like a man I had once known. This being walked over to my bed and laid upon me. He began to kiss my neck and down my shoulder when, suddenly, I pushed him onto his back and sat up. I looked at him and immediately declared that he was not who he said he was. In that moment, his face revealed his true identity and his demonic features were like that of a being with no skin, only muscle and only blood. His head shook left and right as he attempted to leave, but I screamed out the name of Jesus.

"You are not my husband and I rebuke you in the name of Jesus. I rebuke you in the name of Jesus. I rebuke you in the name of Jesus!" I began to flick my hands towards his face and, as I did, Holy Water began pouring out my fingertips, and as the water hit his face, he began to melt into the bed. Smoke filled the room as I watched his face melt in front of me. I rebuked him until there was nothing left of him but a small, red t-shirt, which I picked up and disposed of outside of the room. I woke up with a long gasp for air and laid there in amazement.

He was gone.

Upon this deliverance, I bowed to my Heavenly Father for delivering me. There is no way that I would have known such a curse was upon me if it wasn't for Him. I bask in His glory and I praise His name. He could see every single curse I picked up, whether it was from my life or my ancestors' lives. He could see what was on me and leading me into this fast was crucial because, as much as I wanted to rush ahead with the next chapter of my life, and as much as I wanted to work for the Lord and create a ministry for Him, He knew that all of these curses and strongholds on my life would consistently destroy and take away anything I tried to make work. He knew that if I got close to what I was trying to do, these demons would come in and take everything away. He had to deliver me first before I was able to step into my ministry.

OUT OF THE PIT

It was a Wednesday night at 9:33pm to be precise, when the root of all my evil was revealed to me: the one who opened the door to all cardinal demons – Satan himself. As I was tucking myself into the pages of 'Why Revival Tarries' by Leonard Ravenhill, I was met with the description of a bottomless pit of hell. As I read these words, I found my body freeze. A bottomless pit in hell? That seemed eerily familiar.

Upon doing some research, I discovered that the bottomless pit described in Revelations was a pit I had seen once before. I sat with the word and processed what the Holy Spirit was showing me – the feeling that I had experienced from a young age, that I would describe as a feeling of floating in space, never being able to come to Earth, but also never being able to die. Now it seemed like it had a name that matched the name I had also given it: the abyss. This is the bottomless pit, a place where demons are held and where Satan shall be bound for a thousand years.

And the fifth angel blew his trumpet, and I saw a star fallen from heaven to earth, and he was given the key to the shaft of the bottomless pit.

Revelation 9:1

I had been plagued by this feeling of an abyss from such a young age that I cannot remember when I hadn't felt it.

Many times it would plague me at night. I would find myself trying to drift off to sleep when, suddenly, I'd find myself in the eerie silence of this abyss, in the feeling of space, floating. There was darkness all around me, but I was not able to come back home and I'd never be able to die.

Sometimes this feeling would arise in the morning. I have memories of sitting on my parents' bed, as all of us children did on a Saturday morning – laughing, giggling, and talking about the day – when the feeling of the abyss would wash over me. This feeling was so haunting that I could feel the hairs on my neck rise. The longer I went on feeling it, the more I wanted to run away from it. In fact, I did. So many times in so many different ways. I moved home over and over again. I moved countries and travelled as much as I could, hoping that the emptiness wasn't there when I arrived, though it always was. People would describe me as a feather, always floating, whilst others saw me as a dove, always looking for land to settle on. I wasn't just feeling the abyss, I had become it. But mark the day, I was being delivered.

That night, I was woken at 3.30am with the feeling of this abyss more than ever. As I lay there, feeling the coldness wash through my body and the dread in my heart, I knew I was being delivered.

It was leaving, the Holy Spirit told me. Stand and worship.

I obeyed and rose from my bed to place my hands in the air and sing my praises to the almighty God for exposing the demons that had worked from their bottomless pit to torment me all the days of my life. I sang, I praised and I worshiped.

I wept with gratitude and knelt with humbleness. I bowed to Jesus in gratitude and found myself singing a holy thank you.

"Thank you, Jesus, thank you, Jesus, thank you, Jesus," I repeated.

As I climbed back into bed, the eerie feeling fading into the distance, I slept in the arms of peace.

From that night, I was sealed to God's side. His assignment over my life was so important that even Satan himself sought after me. I could see things in people that were unexplainable and the power that I had to see the demons in people and deliver them was earth shattering. He found me at such a young age, as he does with you and your children because of our vulnerability. You are powerless at this age. Trapped with no way out. As his demons grow in you, so do your illnesses, and you may find labels for them. ADHD is one. It seeks attention and is your excuse for why you can't follow the calling on your life. Bipolar is another. A complete upward and downward distraction from such assignment. Most diagnoses are a bed for your demons to get comfortable. Give them a name and now they're your friend. God delivers you from enemies, not friends, so you can be assured that your label is your invitation for them to stay.

The demons wave cardinal sin flags as pride flags. Satan is the prince of confusion and confusing you or your child as to what they are or who they lust after. Wearing a badge of honour hides the seal of shame that Satan has on your life. If you open your eyes, you'll surely see him. He's in the illness. He's in the confusion. He's in the longing for a person. He's in the distraction. He's in the mess. He's in the filth. He's in the distress. If you open your eyes, you'll see him.

Sealed

IN GREAT HUMILITY

We can separate the true encounters of Jesus from the false ones remarkably easily, because there's no way that one can have this experience and continue doing what you were once doing. Once we've been forgiven ourselves, we cannot hold grudges against our friends and family or even a stranger. We cannot walk in bitterness or anger. The only walk with Him is humility. True encounters bring fruitful changes, the false ones create no change at all.

I do hear the occasional story of people claiming to have met Him, yet their lives remain the same. They stay within the occult, they continue to search the globe for healing modalities, they continue to dishonour their parents, and the list goes on.

These unique individuals met Satan, not Jesus.

And no wonder! For Satan himself transforms himself into an angel of light.

2 Corinthians 11:14

"There is nothing that you can do to make me love you any less," I said to my sister shortly after my fast had ended. "It's a privilege to stand with you through everything. Whatever you need, I'm there. Even if it's 2am, I'm there. You never have to worry about being alone." I couldn't help but notice that the way I was now treating those around me was how my Heavenly Father treated me.

How can I not extend grace when He always extends it to me? I was once a woman who locked herself away. She didn't like people and she'd rather be alone. She saw the trauma in everyone and scuttled to the darkest room to reside as often as she could. She didn't know that the longer you walk with Satan, the more you become like him. The need for solitude is a gift from the Lord, used by the enemy. The desire to live the life of a recluse was within me, as it was my time to be just Him and I, but as the enemy used it against me I felt more and more alone rather than nourished in such times of solitude. Of course, I knew not what Satan's many masks were, therefore I was the same as all the other New Agers. I had fallen for his lies and deception, and I simply didn't think he existed. I was deathly wrong. His mark was all over my life, I just didn't know what it looked like in order to see it. But now, I do. Pride.

"Are you not tired of carrying the burden of being right?" my Heavenly Father once asked me.

After that prayer, I began to see the pride that was in my life. I saw the parts of me that felt I were right, therefore someone else was wrong. I held people to a standard that I could barely keep myself, and if that person should step a toe out of line, there was no mercy. They were dead to me. I didn't speak to them. I cut them off completely. How traumatic.

For many nights I prayed for mercy and wisdom, knowing full well what it's like for someone to just remove themselves from my life. No longer did I want to live a life as a disappearing act; but instead, as a woman with grace. I humbled myself to those who had hurt me in the past and pleaded apologies for my own wrongdoing, because I couldn't see them from any other eyes than His.

I once received some criticism for doing a thing like this. I was told that I was in the right and that I shouldn't apologise. But I couldn't help it. My pride was lifted and I knew nothing else but humility. The vessel that the Holy Spirit was now dwelling in – me – didn't carry the pain that I once had. There was no room to be right or to be better. In fact, in a world that wants to level up, I now wish to bow down.

I spent so many years of my life trying to be better. I was a keen transformationalist and that word always enticed me. Coaches around me encouraged me to level up and transform my life, and I did, so many times. But I was also left in the dirt every time. I may have told people that my life was improving, but under the surface it was getting worse. How can we search for healing without searching for trauma? How can we look at trauma without being traumatised? How can we be traumatised and at the same time see people in the best light? What we don't see, in a world full of people trying to always be better, is that pride leads the way and we don't see ourselves through the eyes of our Lord.

The more I searched for healing, the more I found Satan waiting for me. This search made me hate people more and more and I could see the bitterness of my face on occasions. But this is what Jesus saved me from. No longer could I walk in the shoes of being right or better. I now want quite the opposite. I want to be wrong. I want to learn. I want to forgive and I hold others to no standard other than that which they set themselves.

The more I loved people, the more I realised how much He loved me. It made me see that He loved me no matter what my past was. I was forgiven.

HOLY FIRE

I didn't know what to expect on the other side of my fast. I knew that the Lord was preparing me for some kind of movement, but I didn't know what that was, nor did I know what it looked like. But I believe that He calls us to the unknown so that we may lean on Him every step of the way.

What I received on the other side was the anguish of the Holy Fire. I couldn't help but notice sorrow in my eyes upon glancing in the mirror. Not worldly sadness, but holy sadness, the way our Lord and saviour must have felt. There was a burning sensation in my stomach urging me to preach and teach the word, and now I couldn't stop. I was anointed with the Holy Fire and the ability to speak in tongues was upon me. I was sealed by the Holy Spirit and my full immersion baptism was close by.

As my forty-day fast grew to a close, I could feel its toll. On the outside, I'd chosen a bow for my hair and dressed myself appropriately for the day. I walked with a smile as the Lord beamed His sunlight onto my face. But on the inside, I was crawling, using my fingertips to drag my body across the desert; I was exhausted. After adding three days here and three days there of no food at all, my body was feeling the effects. I knew, though, that it was the only way for me to be delivered from all that I had gathered in my basket over my lifetime. My body felt light and I spent the last week catching my breath and reflecting on the war that I had faced with the Lord.

As I felt the relief, I couldn't help but think that, surely, I could eat normally once again because, surely, it was now over. I was tempted to have a small meal one night despite the fact that I'd had my meal that day. I had been unwell previously and my body needed strength. However, I fought the flesh and reminded myself of the promise I had made to my Heavenly Father, and if He can always keep His promises, then so can I. After going to bed ravenous, I was woken up to the Lord's voice. I adore it when that happens.

He pointed out to me the temptation to break my fast a week early was a temptation of Satan, who didn't want me to step into the calling that the Lord had put on my life. That morning, the Lord invited me to sit with Him so that He could show me what He wanted me to do. He showed me that, in completing my fast, it now gave me authority to walk others down the same path, in His name and for His glory. A whole world opened up to me in which I was myself spending time with individuals who were being called to ministry. I would coach them, fast with them, deliver them and pray with them, all for His glory.

In that moment, I could see why Satan had tempted me to end my fast early, for if I could not walk this path for forty days, I could not lead any other person down it. If I had broken my fast, it would have opened the door for Satan to destroy the beginning of this ministry. It is by the grace of God that I made it through and I thank Him that He delivered me from evil, knowing that I could not step into my calling without first being rid of all that held me back.

If we don't fight the spiritual battle, nothing changes, so I'm always excited when someone knocks on my inbox, ready to fight the battle instead of complaining about it, for so many would rather just take the medicine rather than remove the demon hovering over them as a sickness. But then they are so surprised when the disease enters their body another way.

One of the ways that Satan fights this particular battle himself is to put the fire of the people out. He makes them placid and fed up. They have no fight left in them to live or to die, they merely exist. They shuffle off to work every morning for a small wage. Their heads hang low as they scroll through content on their devices. These videos seem far more exciting than their own lives. Either that or they just need distraction. The whole world is distracted and it's time to wake up because you're missing it. You're missing Him. He's trying to talk to you but you can't hear Him because the music is too loud.

So often people can spot a problem in their life, causing two things to happen. They bury their head, avoid it more, then lie to themselves that it'll be different next year. Or they start to try to get out ahead of it and make some changes in their world. But neither works. We have to fight everything spiritually first, for the war is not on this Earth, it's against it. The war is between heaven and hell, and until we fight that battle, we cannot seek change.

There was a time where I felt very ashamed that I was in the New Age. I felt ashamed that I had dabbled in witchcraft and I felt ashamed that I had played around with tarot cards and spells. This was the deliverance that the Lord had to bring me through, as the enemy so often tried to use my past against me, because it's Satan who makes us feel ashamed. It's him who tries to make us feel guilty for the paths that we've walked down. But something that was apparent to me later on, was that God was with me the whole time. He'd never choose for me the path I went down, but He did allow it to happen and He used it for His glory in the end. He allowed me to get lost because, in getting lost, He was preparing me for my ministry. Because of being in the New Age, I learned a lot about demonic forces and how they operate, giving me a unique point of view. I learned about the abilities of healing and, even though it was the wrong way because Jesus is the only way, it still taught me how to look deep within, how to see in the dark, how to build a business, and how to work with clients. It reminds me that no one has ever strayed too far for Jesus.

He chose me and called me by name and, since that moment, I've followed Him. He has shown me the life that is possible with Him and, as I have walked in faith, not by sight, I have gotten to witness miracles; this book being one of them. For three years I have strived over a book. It was edited a few times and re-written several times. No one wanted to publish it. Once Eli was saved, I thank the Lord for never allowing it to hit the shelves, for I'd certainly be recalling it now. The day I stepped into my forty days fast, He told me I'd write another book. I was filled with dread to begin with, because all I saw was another three years of my life again, slogging away at the keypad, only to get nowhere. Except, this time, He showed me another way. His way.

"Let me show you what I can do," He said.

I could see clearly that the entire book could be written in forty days, and so it was. You're reading it.

I was exhilarated and ready for the Holy Spirit and Holy Fire to work in me and to see this book written. Not that I really wrote this. He did. Whenever I sat to write when He hadn't called me to the keypad, I sat there lost like a bird flying around with no place to land. But when He called me, I would write for hours and be amazed at what was being written. The experience that you've just had reading this, I also had as He wrote through me.

God is good, and as soon as we say 'yes' to a call from Him, he says, "let there be light" and fills us with the Holy Spirit.

I said my 'yes', I paid the price and I've never looked back. I'm not unique or special in any way, and the Lord has not given me anything that He cannot give anyone else, I'm simply a woman who said 'yes' to the call and, soon, He may call you, if you remember that the saved will be called but the called must first be saved. In my salvation, the Lord rid me of bondage both spiritually and physically. He rid me of curses on my life that had been stuck there for generations, and many were not planted by me but by my ancestors. He closed all doors that were open to demonic oppression and protected me as I went through each deliverance, for each deliverance left me more and more exhausted.

As everything begins first in the spiritual, the breaking of such bondage then allowed Him to break the bondage on my physical life too: debt. Debt is a way of keeping us controlled by outward circumstances such as loans and payment plans of any form, as you're a slave to a monthly debt and you're never quite free. My Heavenly Father refused to have me with that life for it's not of Him. I was now His and my life needed to reflect that. My heart certainly did and there would just be no way that my Heavenly Father would sieve out the impurities in me and then leave me in the life that the impurities created. No, He saved me completely.

> **From now on, let no one trouble me, for I bear on my body the marks of Jesus.**
> ***Galatians 6:17***

My Heavenly Father delivered me from my chaotic and lonely life to a life that reflected Him and His kingdom. In the eighteen months of salvation preceding this book, I had very little physically. I gave up the money I had been making in the New Age, as it wasn't from Him, and this left me with nothing. I had to give up my home as I couldn't afford the bills or the rent, and instead I leant on the salvation of the Lord and friends. From the moment I said 'yes' to the calling He had for me, He began His work; and after forty days of seeking Him.

BE NOT AFRAID

We don't need to be afraid of the enemy for he has no power over us. As I heeded the call forward, I of course felt the presence of the enemy, trying to make me focus on him. But I chose not to. Others can choose this also. Of course it is common to be afraid, and I can see a deep fear of warfare in others. But, although we must be aware of it, God calls us to not focus there. I know this because I have been through deep warfare myself and, once it was over, I found myself praying to see joy. I prayed to my Heavenly Father and asked Him to show me the kingdom and the contentment that comes with it, and His first invitation was to no longer face the enemy but instead to face Him and only Him. As I did, I began to feel the lightness of His yoke and the freedom we have in His name. When we're chosen, we inherit Him and His kingdom, therefore we are safe in His arms.

> **Submit yourselves, then, to God. Resist the devil, and he will flee from you.**
>
> ***James 4:7***

No longer did I have to survive. I could rest in His arms and bask in His glory. The assignment He handed to me was nothing short of a miracle and, as I began to minister to women once again, He gave me the opportunity to lead them through what I went through in this book, breaking them of strongholds and the lies of the enemy.

Women all over the world are now being set free because I decided to say 'yes' to the Lord. Our purpose is not about us, it's about those the Lord sends to us to help. Thus, in a way, my 'yes' had little to do with me and a lot to do with them… with you.

Your own 'yes' also has little to do with you and more to do with finding others with the potential to also say 'yes'. For we cannot be selfish. So many are afraid of their calling, but our love for people will override any fear that we have and will pull us through any deliverance that has to happen.

To be afraid of what we know God is calling us to, and not doing it, is against gospel thinking. Even Jesus Himself asked God in the garden of Gethsemane (Matthew 26:39) if He'd spare Him and if there was a different way to save humanity other than the pain He was about to endure. He suffered for us anyway and accepted God's plan. We must also.

So, the next time God sends someone into your life to nudge you into the calling that you know is yours, listen. Be not afraid. Don't walk away. But instead, be in obedience.

When I could, the one question that I asked Jesus was, 'why are my hands so heavy'. His response was: 'that is the burden of the cross.' Your calling is your cross and how dare we pray in thanks that He died for us but say 'no' to our own cross! I wouldn't dare dream of such disrespect to the Heavenly Father and I pray, in the name of Jesus, that you'll pick up your cross and walk with it.

The Assignment

BRING MY CHILDREN HOME

The assignment that my Heavenly Father gave to me was to 'go back to the places you once were and bring my children home.' As time went on, this began to translate in front of me as I was found by people who were tied up with their own curses and oppressions, and by women who had strongholds with men in their past. They had no value for themselves and they were dripping in poverty posed as diamonds. They knew they had a calling, but were distracted by the world. The authority that the Lord gave me was to pull them through what He pulled me through, so that they could understand and find the land that the Lord had waiting for them.

Thus here I am now, walking boldly in the truth of Jesus. I take the hands of women from all over the world and walk them to the land that the Lord has for them. When they get there, they're in awe of His splendour and grace – that this is what He had for them all along. This is their land; their assignment. They are home.

One thing I tell all those who find me in search of their own calling in life is that when you find it, your whole life will make sense. As I look back, I can see the training ground through which my Heavenly Father walked me. I see how it taught me to speak a certain way, listen a certain way and teach a certain way. I can also see how all these traits were things I hid from others and disliked in myself.

At first, I was so on fire for the Lord that it sometimes offended people, and I was so afraid to step back out into the world. I had a boldness to me that many friends pointed out. I always had. I had always wanted to move in the opposite direction of the world, because the direction of the world just didn't make sense to me, and it certainly didn't make sense that people were selling their time for money, which they then used to pay for things they rarely got to use because they were always selling their time.

Coming out of my forty-day fast, the Lord began to show me the land that He had for me. Morning, noon and night I studied the word of God and was met with patterns and principles that I'd never seen before. I was blown away by how often the Lord had land for those He chose and, when the land was ready, He called the person to it and, just like Abraham, when the call came I went in obedience and without haste.

The Lord had said to Abram, "Go from your country, your people and your father's household to the land I will show you.

I will make you into a great nation, and I will bless you; I will make your name great, and you will be a blessing.

**I will bless those who bless you,
and whoever curses you I will curse;
and all peoples on earth
will be blessed through you."**

So Abram went, as the Lord had told him; and Lot went with him.

Genesis 12:1

As I studied the work of God, I noticed that when God calls on someone's life, He always prepares it for them *and then* calls them to it. The world does the opposite. People tend to chase what they perceive should be their destination, or things within that perceived destination, and attempt to create it for themselves. But this is not the way God calls us.

I saw this exact same experience scattered throughout Genesis. Only once God had land for Abraham did He call him to pack up his things and leave. Our Heavenly Father has land for us all and so many of us feel the call, but don't know what to do with it.

However, I was starting to see the land that He had for me, and as my Heavenly Father began to reveal that land, it was beyond what my mind could ever imagine. As I gazed upon it, I couldn't help but feel ashamed for once thinking I had ever known what I needed. In fact, I was almost embarrassed that I once believed I could manifest something so priceless all by myself, for what He showed me made my old little dreams look insignificant and disjointed.

Thankfully, I now lived in obedience and where He called me, I went. As the months went on and the veil unravelled,

I was met with a movement inspired by John 13:8, in which I saw myself greatly. Just like Peter, I felt unworthy for Jesus to wash my feet. But if we don't let Him, we have no part of Him. The Lord was calling me to wash as many feet as possible, in many different ways, and as He said, 'bring His children home.'

The more I said 'yes' to His call, the more protection I felt from my Heavenly Father. I began to see that, when we're in our God-given calling, we are shielded, for such a purpose is not about us but about those we are called to serve. My entire fast and salvation was not about me, but about those whose feet I would wash. Within this calling, I felt the protection of the firmament that God created over His world and, within that, I was safe to move, grow and teach in the name of the Lord. I began to make online content to expose the world I once lived in and right before my eyes, I saw more and more people wake up to Jesus.

That summer, I had my full immersion baptism. This was my public declaration to the Lord and how I was His and only His. Anyone who wanted to know me had to first know Him. The weeks leading up to this were precious and intimate. I fasted the week leading up to it and the week after and basked in the glory of the King. Soon after, I met face to face with who God truly made me to be. Not a boss, not a business woman, not a survivor but instead, a creator. An artist. A woman who could recognise a beautiful fabric when she saw it and who could see the beauty that God began with. Heaven is really on earth and the Kingdom is really here, locked away safely for only those who are born again can see.

Like a child, my days began as they once did before the enemy took me. I spent my mornings making sure my bow matched the frill on my sock so that I could sit with my paint brushes as God always intended. Day by day, paintings of the man who saved me went onto papers, canvases and boards and day by day, they were being sold and sent around the world to wash the feet of their owners. The 13:8 Movement became something of its very own and created by God, not me, I began to see that we were washing the feet of the nations.

ALL FOR HIM

I'd have made a great wife. I'm focused, dedicated and loyal. I enjoy taking care of people. I would have enjoyed taking care of a man. But relationships never seemed to be a great success in my life. I believe in a woman submitting to a man and allowing him to be the leader of the home, as I see that when roles are reversed we witness strife and chaos. I also recognise how sick a woman can become if the man doesn't speak to her softly, hold her lovingly and treat her tenderly. I've experienced pieces of this but never did a man reach into the depth of the heart I carried, leaving that perpetual loneliness rattling within me.

When Jesus appeared to me in my room, there was one thing that stood out later on. All of what He did lined up with scripture; the washing of the feet, the cleansing of the blood and the anointing with oil. All of this offered forgiveness and broke chains. But there was something He did that I don't see in the scripture – He looked at me. My torment from a young age, as a girl carrying heavenly gifts without realising it and as a woman with a heart deeper than the ocean, I felt invisible as if no one could see me. I felt like a woman reading the sonnets of Heaven, yet as I read, no one heard. This torment I carried on my shoulders until the day I met our Christ and, on that day, it shall not go unnoticed, that He took the time to see me, washing me free from the torment of invisibility and spoiling me for any other man. As He held my face, He looked deep within my eyes, causing the empty places to be filled with the Holy Spirit and the light of His glory. Therefore I declare a chaste life.

This is something so sacred to me that I daren't speak of it long. Just as a husband and wife should keep their life private from others, I vow to keep my commitments to the Lord between He and I, not just because it's precious, but because speaking to others, whether strangers or friends, about those we love, the problems we may be having or the beauty we may be witnessing, allows room for the enemy to destroy it, and I've seen too many marriages fall apart when sacred things are shared.

Sacred things belong in velvet boxes, locked away in a vault that is hidden deep in the Kingdom to protect its holiness. It would be arrogant of me to think I can make someone understand this choice of life, but there is no other way. I've witnessed the living Christ and been called into an apostleship. I can only be with Him and I can only be understood by Him. Many other rooms that I walk in, I am misunderstood, and sometimes without saying anything I am offensive. But I can't help it. His glory is in me. He washed me with His blood and anointed me with oil. I am His bride.

After being in the presence of Jesus Himself, I am spoiled for any other man. It allowed me to see how so many who long for love and marriage are, in fact, seeking the Lord. You don't need a man, you need Jesus.

I bow my head in grace, humbleness and gratitude for the golden seal that Jesus has placed on my life. He bought me at a price. Signed for, am I, the daughter of the Most High. Sealed am I, protected by the blood of Jesus Christ. Delivered am I, by the Holy Spirit and baptised am I, of the Holy Fire. Now, able only to serve. Now, breathing only for Him. Now, living in anticipation, waiting for His next call.

It is finished.

After this, Jesus, knowing that all things were now accomplished, that the Scripture might be fulfilled, said, "I thirst!" Now a vessel full of sour wine was sitting there; and they filled a sponge with sour wine, put it on hyssop, and put it to His mouth. So when Jesus had received the sour wine, He said, "It is finished!" And bowing His head, He gave up His spirit.

John 19:28-30

ACKNOWLEDGEMENTS

From the time I was saved, the Lord placed me into the hands of friends and strangers who became friends. They took care of me whilst I went through the process of giving up my business, finances and home all so that I could build a new life that glorified God. To them, I owe a big thank you for their generosity and kindness. My friend Duchess who inspired me with her fragrant perspective of life and Phyllis who gave me a place to stay when there was nowhere else to go, I thank you.

Finally, a gracious bow is owed to my dear friend Hailey, who has never failed to protect my steps. When others didn't want me, she did. She is there for the tears and the laughs, always reminding me to celebrate my achievements and helping me to pick up the pieces any time life got fractured. Never judged by her and always loved, her hugs have got me through many times of despair.

ABOUT THE AUTHOR

Laura Ansell is a writer, speaker and teacher. She is the founder of *Finding your Flock* where she ministers to women globally to pick up their cross and walk. She frees them from the rat race of the world and turns them into leading entrepreneurs where they can claim the calling that God has for them. Her mission here is to bring as many as she can into their life purpose to serve the works of our Lord.

She is also the leader of the *13:8 Movement* where she shares her story of being face to face with Jesus to win souls for the kingdom.

Read more about her work at *lauraansell.co.uk*

www.ingramcontent.com/pod-product-compliance
Lightning Source LLC
Chambersburg PA
CBHW071211070526
44584CB00019B/2994